3 $\frac{38}{}$

BENJAMIN FRANKLIN *& Polly Baker*

The Institute of Early American History and Culture is sponsored jointly by the College of William and Mary and Colonial Williamsburg, Incorporated. Publication of this book has been assisted by a grant from the Lilly Endowment, Inc.

BENJAMIN FRANKLIN.
Né à Boston dans la nouvelle Angleterre le 17 Janvier 1706.

BENJAMIN FRANKLIN
By Joh. Martin Will after the 1777 portrait by C. N. Cochin.

Benjamin Franklin
& POLLY BAKER

The
History of a Literary Deception

 BY MAX HALL

PUBLISHED FOR
The Institute of Early American History and Culture
AT WILLIAMSBURG, VIRGINIA
By The University of North Carolina Press, Chapel Hill

To Elizabeth

PREFACE

M Y investigation of the Polly Baker affair has been my
hobby for nearly ten years. Whenever I seemed to
be near publication, Polly suddenly showed up somewhere
new. Many persons helped in the chase. I am indebted
to two of them most of all. One is Arthur M. Schlesinger,
Sr., of Harvard University, who advised and encouraged
me from the beginning and criticized the manuscript in two
of its metamorphoses. My interest in Franklin began when
I was a Nieman Fellow at Harvard, on leave from the job
I then held in the Washington bureau of the Associated
Press. The other is Whitfield J. Bell, Jr., associate editor of
The Papers of Benjamin Franklin, who, in a correspondence
of several years, generously supplied much new information
about Polly Baker which he uncovered in his search for
Franklin papers.

I am also grateful to Clifford K. Shipton and Jack C.
Barnes; to Verner W. Crane and Alfred Owen Aldridge; to
Herbert Dieckmann, Frederick B. Tolles, Rudolph Elie, and
Mary Moore Molony, all of whom went out of their way to
contribute something of value. Most of them are further
mentioned in my text and notes. Carl Van Doren wrote me
a keen and amusing letter about Polly shortly before his
death. Others, too numerous to list, were kind enough to
reply to my questions.

Preface

Most of the research took place in the Harvard College Library, the New York Public Library, the Library of Congress, and the British Museum, though I visited about fifteen other libraries for special purposes and received information or photostats from still others.

My wife, Elizabeth, and our children, Clay, Nancy, and Judith, made the book possible by their helpfulness in many ways, especially their patience when Polly monopolized my evenings, weekends, and vacations. Finally, I wish to thank my mother, Minerva Hall, who, as a writer, gave me an early inclination in that direction.

MAX HALL
Crestwood, New York

CONTENTS

ILLUSTRATIONS

BENJAMIN FRANKLIN   *frontispiece*

The French caption beneath Franklin's name reads "Born
in Boston in New England, January 17, 1706." The likeness
is by Joh. Martin Will after the 1777 portrait by C. N.
Cochin. (Courtesy of The Metropolitan Museum of Art,
Bequest of Charles Allen Munn, 1924.)

GENTLEMAN'S MAGAZINE, APRIL 1747   *facing page* 17

Polly Baker's speech is listed in the table of contents. This
was its first appearance in a magazine.

TITLE PAGE OF SOCIAL BLISS CONSIDERED   *facing page* 51

Under the pseudonym of "Gideon Archer" this pamphlet
by Peter Annet was published in 1749, two years after the
initial appearance of Polly Baker's speech. (Courtesy of
the Vassar College Library.)

BENJAMIN FRANKLIN & *Polly Baker*

CHAPTER *One*

Meet Miss Baker

O N the fifteenth day of April in the year 1747, one of London's leading daily newspapers, the *General Advertiser,* printed a courtroom speech which it said had been delivered by a woman who was being prosecuted for the fifth time for bearing a bastard child. The newspaper said the trial had taken place "at *Connecticut* near *Boston* in *New-England."* The defendant's name was Polly Baker. Her words were far more eloquent than one would normally expect from a woman with such a police record. The *General Advertiser* reported that the speech had influenced the court to dispense with a penalty and had induced one of the judges to marry her the next day.

The publication of this story on April 15 produced an explosive chain reaction in the British periodical press. During the next few days "The Speech of Miss Polly Baker" showed up in at least **five** London newspapers and was copied in other British cities. At the end of April, London's three monthly magazines lent their circulations to Miss Baker's stirring plea. A magazine in Edinburgh printed it. So did one in Dublin. When copies of the English periodicals reached America by sailing vessel in July, the speech was promptly picked up by newspapers in Boston, New York, and Annapolis. No doubt it would have appeared in American magazines, too, had any existed at the time. Four had been founded during the 1740's, including one by Benjamin Franklin, but they had all flickered and failed before 1747.

Thus, without benefit of telegraph or wireless or any Associated Press, the triumph of Polly Baker was publicized with impressive speed throughout the English-reading world. All the periodicals, copying gleefully from one another in the manner of that century, reported the speech as an authentic occurrence, though they were regrettably inexact about the "where" and "when" of the trial. In Chapters 2, 3, and 4 we will look more closely at them, especially the *General Advertiser,* the *Gentleman's Magazine,* and the *Maryland Gazette* because of the extraordinary and puzzling circumstances of their presentations. Now let us see what it was, according to the *General Advertiser,* that Miss Baker told her judges.

Polly described herself as a poor unhappy woman who had no money to pay lawyers. She reminded the judges that this was the fifth time she had been dragged before them on a similar charge; twice she had paid heavy fines and twice been whipped in public. She admitted breaking the law but declared that the law was unreasonable in itself and particularly severe with regard to her, who had never wronged man, woman, or child. Aside from this law, she said, she could not conceive what the nature of her offense had been.

"I have brought Five fine Children into the World," said Polly, "at the Risque of my Life; I have maintain'd them well by my own Industry, without burthening the Township, and would have done it better, if it had not been for the heavy Charges and Fines I have paid. Can it be a Crime (in the Nature of Things I mean) to add to the Number of the King's Subjects, in a new Country that really wants People?"

Polly denied that she had ever debauched any woman's husband or enticed any youth. She said nobody had the least cause of complaint against her, unless perhaps a minister or a justice of the peace, because he had missed a wedding fee. But could this be a fault of hers? She would prefer wedlock, and was always willing to enter into it, "and doubt not my behaving well in it, having all the Industry, Frugality, Fertility, and Skill in Oeconomy, appertaining to a good Wife's Character."

Polly defied anyone to say she had ever refused a bona fide proposal of marriage. On the contrary, she had readily consented to the only one she had ever received, which was when she was a virgin, "but too easily confiding in the Person's Sincerity that made it," said she, "I unhappily lost my own Honour, by trusting to his; for he got me with Child, and then forsook me." She told the judges that they all knew her betrayer, for he had now become a magistrate. She had hoped that he would appear today on the bench and try to influence the court in her favor, but he did not, and therefore she must complain that it was unjust and unequal for this man (whom she did not name) to be advanced to honor and power in the government that punished her misfortunes with stripes and infamy.

Then Polly turned to another aspect of the case. "If mine, then, is a religious Offence," she said, "leave it to religious Punishments. You have already excluded me from the Comforts of your Church-Communion. Is not that sufficient? You believe I have offended Heaven, and must suffer eternal Fire: Will not that be sufficient? What Need is there, then, of your additional Fines and Whipping? ... But, how can it be believed, that Heaven is angry at my having Children, when to the little done by me towards it, God has been pleased to add his Divine Skill and admirable Workmanship in the Formation of their Bodies, and crown'd it, by furnishing them with rational and immortal Souls."

Polly told the judges that if they must be making laws, let them not "turn natural and useful Actions into Crimes," but take into their wise consideration the great and growing number of bachelors, who, by their manner of living, were leaving unproduced "Hundreds of their Posterity to the Thousandth Generation." This she said was "little better than Murder," and the bachelors should be compelled either to marry or to pay double the fine of fornication every year.

Miss Polly Baker, according to the *General Advertiser,* concluded:

What must poor young Women do, whom Custom have forbid to solicit the Men, and who cannot force themselves upon Husbands, when the Laws take no Care to provide them any; and yet severely punish them if they do their Duty without them; the Duty of the first and great Command of Nature, and of Nature's God, *Encrease and Multiply.* A Duty, from the steady Performance of which, nothing has been able to deter me; but for its Sake, I have hazarded the Loss of the Publick Esteem, and have frequently endured Publick Disgrace and Punishment; and therefore ought, in my humble Opinion, instead of a Whipping, to have a Statue erected to my Memory.[1]

Englishmen neither knew nor cared much about the wild and remote regions across the Atlantic where Polly Baker was said to have delivered her five offspring and her oration. The colonies were only gradually acquiring the population, the American outlook, and the divergences from British interests that finally led to the break when sufficient provocations occurred. In 1747, George Washington was fifteen years old, John Adams was twelve, Jefferson was only four, and Madison and Hamilton were not yet born. Benjamin Franklin, at the age of forty-one, had already piled up a fortune in the printing and publishing business. He was happily engaged in electrical experiments, and these experiments were soon to make him the first American to attain world renown. But even Franklin was unknown to the English public on the April day when Polly Baker became famous in London.

Complacency was a prevailing mood in the England of that time. The period has been described as prosaic, commonplace, unwashed, and unsavory. From another viewpoint, it has been called a merciful moment of quiet between past religious fanaticisms and future fanaticisms of other kinds.[2]

1. *General Advertiser,* April 15, 1747. The complete text of the speech as printed there is given in the Appendix, pp. 157-67.
2. Francis Parkman, quoted in Donald Sheehan, ed., *The Making of American History* (New York, 1950), 34-35; G. M. Trevelyan, *English Social History* (London, 1943), 339.

If these mid-century years were unspectacular they were nevertheless in a condition of interesting pregnancy. The Industrial Revolution was beginning to take shape. Though aristocratic influence remained strong, the middle classes grew steadily in numbers and importance, and they hungered after instruction and diversion. The printing-houses, strung out to the north and west of St. Paul's Cathedral in London, issued an expanding stream of books, plays, pamphlets, sermons, broadsides, magazines, and newspapers. And authors had become capable of writing with sympathy about ordinary people, including shopkeepers and maid-servants, and even about the lowest strata of society.

In fact, some of England's best literary men had dealt with the subject of fallen women and the males who had contributed to their fall. The pace had been set in 1711 and 1712 by "Mr. Spectator," which is to say by Steele and Addison, two of the greatest pace-setters in the history of literature. Richard Steele, instead of savagely attacking harlotry, as had been customary for two centuries, devoted several sympathetic essays in the *Spectator* to poor deluded "women of the town" who (like Polly Baker) would much prefer another kind of life. Steele, in the words of H. V. Routh, "reveals, for the first time, the 'white-slave traffic' of his age," with all its fiendish stratagems for sapping the virtue of its dupes, and with its secret patrons among high society.[3] Joseph Addison, for his part, made an onslaught against the "loose Tribe of Men . . . that ramble into all the Corners of this great City, in order to seduce such unfortu-

3. H. V. Routh, "Steele and Addison," in Sir A. W. Ward and A. R. Waller, eds., *Cambridge History of English Literature* (Cambridge, England, 1932), IX, 56. Also see the *Spectator,* Nos. 182, 190, 266, 274, 276.

nate Females as fall into their Walks."[4] He said these "abandoned Profligates raise up Issue in every Quarter of the Town," and "I have heard a Rake who was not quite Five and Twenty declare himself the Father of a Seventh Son." The same essay contains the following noteworthy passage:

Were I to propose a Punishment for this infamous Race of Propagators, it should be to send them, after the second or third Offence, into our *American* Colonies, in order to People those Parts of her Majesty's Dominions where there is a want of Inhabitants, and in the Phrase of *Diogenes* to *Plant Men*. Some Countries punish this Crime with Death; but I think such a Banishment would be sufficient, and might turn this generative Faculty to the Advantage of the Publick.

Addison concluded with an exhortation to the fathers of bastards to take care of these innocent unfortunates and educate them well. One could almost imagine that Polly Baker had read Addison. Conversely, one might imagine that Addison anticipated Miss Baker, for in a later *Spectator* essay on female orators, he wrote: "Were Women admitted to plead in Courts of Judicature, I am persuaded they would carry the Eloquence of the Bar to greater Heights than it has yet arrived at."[5]

Then comes Daniel Defoe, the prolific middle-class journalist, the son of a butcher, and the father or perhaps the grandfather of the English novel, who characterized sexually abandoned women in two notable works of fiction

4. *Spectator,* No. 203, Oct. 23, 1711. These quotations are from the text in *Everyman's Library,* which reprints the *Spectator* in four volumes; No. 203 appears in Vol. II (London, 1907).

5. *Spectator,* No. 247, Dec. 13, 1711.

written to sound like fact. The first, *Moll Flanders* (1722), was the life story of a woman who, for fear of poverty, lost her virtue and went on to prostitution and thievery. Now the name "Moll" has a definite kinship with the name "Polly," since both are corruptions of "Mary." And Moll Flanders had something in common with Polly Baker. Like Polly, she bore several bastards, though she did not equal Polly in maintaining them. Like Polly, she once protested that if she had happened to meet with a sober, good husband, she would have been "as faithful and true a wife to him as virtue itself could have formed." And like Polly, she once delivered a courtroom speech in her own defense.⁶ The other book was *Roxana, or The Fortunate Mistress* (1724), in which Defoe gave us the counterpart of Moll Flanders in a higher social sphere.

Next in this cavalcade of female unfortunates comes another Polly—Polly Peachum of John Gay's hilarious and fabulously successful satire, *The Beggar's Opera,* first produced in 1728. Miss Peachum marries a rascally highwayman with a record of several mistresses and bastards. This marriage confounds her parents, and they abuse her dreadfully, calling her such names as "hussy" and "baggage." Mr. Peachum asks her, "Do you think your mother and I should have lived comfortably so long together, if ever we had been married?" And Mrs. Peachum in a great passion sings an aria that goes:

> Our Polly is a sad slut! nor heeds what we have
> taught her.
> I wonder any man alive will ever rear a daughter!⁷

6. Defoe, *Moll Flanders,* Modern Library edn. (New York, 1950), 119, 272.
7. From the text in George H. Nettleton and Arthur E. Case, eds., *British Dramatists from Dryden to Sheridan* (Boston, 1939), 541.

Now another Baker enters this narrative. The famous *Spectator* of 1711 and 1712 had innumerable imitators. One of the better ones was a weekly essay-newspaper called the *Universal Spectator* which started life in 1728. For more than four years it was managed by an unusual young man named Henry Baker with an assist from the aging Daniel Defoe, who wrote the first issue.[8] The *Universal Spectator* was published under the pen name of "Henry Stonecastle of Northumberland, Esq." It gave its readers, among other things, a good deal of lively female-versus-male controversy of the kind then popular. Henry Baker, in some of the approximately one hundred essays he provided for this paper, carried on a thundering crusade in favor of matrimony, which he himself embraced in 1729 by marrying Defoe's daughter Sophia. And in one of those essays, published on February 13, 1731, Baker used language that bears a curious likeness to certain passages in the speech of Polly Baker as printed sixteen years later.[9]

The first part of his essay was in the form of a petition to Henry Stonecastle from "Rachel Wishful," "Deborah Sprightly," "Susanna Lovemore," and *"Thirty Thousand"* other *"Virgins, Spinsters, Single Women, and Widows in* Great-Britain," whose names were conveniently omitted. The petitioners began by declaring that a multitude of people had always been accounted the truest riches of a kingdom, and that the means of procuring them in all civilized nations had ever been matrimony. The petitioners were

8. George Reuben Potter, "Henry Baker, F. R. S. (1698-1774)," *Modern Philology,* 29 (1932), 301-21.

9. Feb. 13 issue unavailable, but the essays were reprinted in book form under the title *The Universal Spectator;* the quotations are from the third edn. (London, 1756), II, 241-46.

ready to contribute their honest endeavors to the peopling of their country. They were "not sensible of any kind of Impediment in themselves" to prevent their entering into matrimony, but verily believed themselves "duly qualify'd, in all Respects, to discharge the Duties of it." They complained that men, who enjoyed "the sole *Privilege* of professing *Love,* and proposing *Matrimony,*" were making little or no use of the privilege. They said that by this neglect, "your *Petitioners* remain at present wholly unserviceable to their King and Country." And this put them under great uneasiness of mind "for not fulfilling *God*'s first Command, *increase and multiply,* which they believe their indispensible and bounden Duty."

Polly Baker, too, declared herself willing and fully qualified to enter into wedlock, and she, too, spoke warmly of women's duty—"the Duty of the first and great Command of Nature, and of Nature's God, *Encrease and Multiply.*" Polly, however, differed from the petitioners in a very important respect: she obeyed the command.

"Henry Stonecastle," after quoting the "petition," launched into a long, enthusiastic defense of marriage. Like Polly, he proposed a tax on bachelors.

Throughout the thirties, ruined women—or men speaking for them by proxy—continued to regret their ruin for the edification of the public. On June 22, 1731, a new kind of play, a prose tragedy involving middle-class characters, was produced at the Drury Lane Theatre, and it was a hit. This was *The London Merchant: or, the History of George Barnwell,* by George Lillo. The play shows the disastrous results of departing from the path of virtue, and the leading female character, Sarah Millwood, a wanton who sinks as low as murder, does not fail to hurl bitter blame on flattering, faithless, barbarous men who violate maids and rob them of their innocence. She makes several speeches along this line, denouncing priests, "venal magistrates," and indeed all men.[10]

In the following year, 1732, a young artist named William Hogarth published a series of six prints entitled "A Harlot's Progress." These pictures showed the pitiful life and death of a Yorkshire parson's daughter, Mary Hackabout, who came to London and was led astray. They established Hogarth's reputation as a genius. They also brought forth a gush of pamphlets and plays based on the sordid career of Mary Hackabout. That is, of Moll or Polly Hackabout, if one wanted to use the common nicknames.[11]

The periodical press continued to do its part as a vehicle for the laments of betrayed women, fictitious or otherwise. For example, in 1735, after Henry Baker had departed from the *Universal Spectator,* that same sheet printed a long letter purporting to be from "one of those lost unhappy Creatures, falsely call'd *Women of Pleasure."* She declared, "The Laws, which hunt and punish us, wou'd be much juster did they oblige the Traitors, by whom we are first undone, . . . to redress our Wrongs." Then she launched into the sad

10. *The London Merchant: or, the History of George Barnwell,* "By Mr. Lillo," 3rd edn. revised (London, 1731), 18, 58-59, 60.

11. Robert Etheridge Moore, *Hogarth's Literary Relationships* (Minneapolis, 1948), 25-40, describes a pamphlet of verse and a ballad opera, in both of which the harlot is called Moll Hackabout. She is called sometimes "Polly" and sometimes "Margot" in a more recent work in which Hogarth's six prints appear as illustrations. See Guillaume Apollinaire, ed., *L'Œuvre de John Cleland: Memoires de Fanny Hill, Femme de Plaisir* (Paris, 1923), a French edition of a notorious eighteenth-century English novel.

story of how she had been seduced by her father's landlord when she was only fifteen.[12]

It was just a few years later that the English novel, which had made a tentative start with the reportorial Defoe, rumbled unmistakably into motion. And when it did, the first big best-seller was a novel of attempted seduction. This was *Pamela* (1740), written in the epistolary style by Samuel Richardson, the pink, plump, five-foot-five proprietor of a London printing-house. Richardson made the sentimental middle-class readers gasp over the struggles of a poor servant girl, Pamela Andrews, to defend her chastity against the incredibly persistent advances of a young squire, Mr. B.

Pamela was followed in 1742 by the first novel of the brilliant Henry Fielding, journalist, lawyer, and later a distinguished magistrate. This book was *Joseph Andrews.* It starts out to be a parody of *Pamela,* though it becomes much more. Joseph, a handsome footman, is represented to be Pamela's brother, and he is as zealous as she in defending his virtue against all challengers.

In April of 1747, when the speech of Polly Baker dropped into this magnificent decade in the history of the novel, the following activities were in progress:

• Richardson was writing his *Clarissa,* in which the heroine emulates Pamela for nearly 2,000 pages but is finally drugged and violated by her pursuer, a rake named Lovelace.[13]

12. *Universal Spectator,* No. 366, Oct. 11, 1735.

13. *Clarissa* began coming out volume by volume in late 1747 or early 1748; there were seven volumes in all. See John Angus Burrell's introduction to the *Modern Library* edn. (New York, 1950), viii.

- Tobias Smollett, a Scottish surgeon, was preparing for the 1748 publication of his first novel, *Roderick Random,* a rowdy adventure story containing, among many other things, a pitiful story told by a wretched prostitute, Nancy Williams. When she was fifteen she possessed "beauty, good sense, and education," but a man got her with child and forsook her, and that was the beginning of a life of shame.[14]

- Fielding was writing *Tom Jones,* which would be published in 1749. It is the life story of the foundling son of an unmarried mother.[15]

This catalogue of seduction, ruined women, and bastards in the literature of the first half of the eighteenth century is by no means complete, but it is enough to suggest one of the causes of Polly Baker's popularity: readers were conditioned to the subject matter and receptive to it.[16] And it is enough to beget a suspicion, at least as large as a man's hand, that the arguments in Polly's speech were the work of someone who was not a total stranger to English literature.

For all that, her speech was something different in the chronicles of ruined women. It was no mere imitation. It had a fresh American locale and a slyness all its own. Its vitality was to carry it far.

14. The *Everyman's Library* edn. (London, 1927), 122-42. The *Gentleman's Magazine,* 19 (1749), 125, was sufficiently impressed with Miss Williams' speech to quote part of it.
15. George Sherburn, in his introduction to the *Modern Library* edn. (New York, 1950), vii, says the years 1746-1748 seem to be the period of composition.
16. Johan Viktor Johansson, a Swedish scholar, in his *Études sur Denis Diderot* (Göteborg et Paris, 1927), 175, apparently was the first to attribute part of Polly's popularity to the development of a romantic middle class, and to mention Richardson and Lillo in this connection.

CHAPTER *Two*

Polly Captures the British Press

UNWASHED complacent London in the spring of 1747 possessed about fifteen newspapers. Four were dailies.[1] Picture one of these, the *General Advertiser,* in the hands of a reader on Wednesday, April 15, as he settled himself in a London coffeehouse. The sheet was about the size of a modern tabloid, though slightly longer and narrower. It contained four pages, each with three wide columns. No headlines jumped out to shatter the reader's mid-eighteenth-century poise. The first item, headed only, *"Deal, April* 13," stated that a ship named the *Charming Polly* had sailed past Deal, bound for Lisbon. (It is remarkable how many ships of the eighteenth century had "Polly" in their names.) The reader's eye traveled down through a few more scraps of shipping news, then through nearly two columns of advices reporting troop movements on the continent. These paragraphs were credited to "the Mail from Holland" and to

1. F. W. Bateson, ed., *The Cambridge Bibliography of English Literature* (Cambridge, England, 1940), II, 708. Aside from the *General Advertiser,* the dailies were the *Daily Advertiser,* the *Daily Gazetteer,* and the *London Courant.* The April issues of the *Daily Advertiser* show no sign of Polly. As for the other two sheets, the inadequacy of files prevents a conclusive check.

The *Gentleman's Magazine:*

Lond Gazette
Read'g Journ
Craftsman
Daily Adver-
tiser.
St James's E-
vening Post
London Even-
ing Po-
Gen. Evening
Post
Daily Gazet-
teer
Gen. Adver-
tiser
Westminster
Journ-l.
Old England
Anatomist.
Lon. Courant
Whitehall Eb
Post

St JOHN's GATE

York 3 Newp
Dublin 4
Edinburgh 2
Bristol :: 2 ·
Norwich 2
Exeter 2
Worcester
N rthampon
Gloucester 3
Stamford :
Nottingham:
Chester Your
Derby ditto
Ipswich 11
Reading 12
Leeds. Sderc
Newcastle 3
Canterbury
Colchester.
Sherborn
Birmingh m
Manchester
Bath
Cambridge

For A P R I L 1747.

C O N T A I N I N G,

[More in Quantity and greater Variety than any Book of the Kind and Price.]

I. Account of the behaviour and execution of lord *Lovat*, with further particulars of his life.
II. History of *Genoa*, an account of
the expulsion of the *Austrians*, and the
oftentatious inscription on § occasion.
III. Remedy for sizy blood.
IV. Method to prevent ships from
leaking.
V. Method of warming all the rooms
in a house by the kitchen fire, with a cut.
VI. Description of *Iceland* and man-
ners of its inhabitants.
VII. Speech of *Polly Baker*.
VIII. The abbe *de la Ville*'s memorial,
and the *French* king's curious declara-
tion at length to the *Dutch* states.
IX. Essay on female education.
X. Emendation of a passage in *Shakespear*.
XI. Office of a Stadtholder.

XII. Description of *Dutch Brabant*,
and *Dutch Flanders*.
XIII. Letter from the master of *Lovat*,
Mr *Painter*'s letters, with lord *Lovat*'s
remarks on him.
XIV. Electrical experiments pro-
posed, and problems answered.
XV. An account of the taking fort St
George and *Madras*.
XVI. Charge against *Milton* continu'd.
XVII. List of ships taken.
XVIII. Poetry. Specimen of a new
translation of *Tasso*; the father, a tale;
to the duke of *Cumberland*, *French* and
English; in memory of Mr *Chubb*.
XIX. Historical chronicle.
XX. List of births and marriages.
XXI. Each day's price of stocks.
XXII. Foreign history.
XXIII. Register of books.

With a Plan of G E N O A, shewing its remarkable places
by above 100 references, also another curious Plate.

By *S Y L V A N U S U R B A N*, Gent.

LONDON: Printed by E. Cave, jun. at St *John's Gate,*

GENTLEMAN'S MAGAZINE

Title page of the April 1747 issue, listing Polly Baker's speech in
the table of contents.

the official *London Gazette,* and bore such datelines as Genoa, Naples, Leghorn, Vienna, Brussels, and Amsterdam. Next came a string of brief London notices.

About midway in the third column commenced "The SPEECH of Miss POLLY BAKER." We are entitled to imagine that the reader shifted his paper to bring more light on the subject and that when he had turned the page and finished the piece on page two, he uttered an exclamation that startled a gentleman at the next table.

At the bottom of the fourth and last page was the information that the paper was "Printed by W. EGELSHAM, at Mr. *Woodfall's,* near the *Pump* in *Little-Britain."* But there was nothing to indicate where Egelsham or Woodfall obtained the news about Polly Baker's trial. Little Britain was the same picturesque neighborhood where Benjamin Franklin had lived and worked as a journeyman printer in 1725, at age nineteen, during his first residence in London.[2] Wells Egelsham, it seems, was not the real publisher of the *General Advertiser,* but only a compositor in the shop where it was issued. The "Mr. Woodfall" mentioned in the paper was Henry Woodfall, Jr., an important miscellaneous printer who contributed notably to the development of the daily press in England. Five years after introducing Polly Baker's speech he gave his paper a new name, the *Public Advertiser,* under which it achieved great renown among daily newspapers of that century. His son, Henry Sampson Woodfall, was only eight years old when his father printed Polly's discourse; but he should not be dismissed without mentioning

2. Franklin's Autobiography, in Albert Henry Smyth, ed., *The Writings of Benjamin Franklin* (New York, 1905-1907), I, 276-77.

a remarkable fact about his later life as publisher of the *Public Advertiser*. Between 1765 and 1775 he printed about forty pieces by Benjamin Franklin. During this period Franklin, in London, made the *Public Advertiser* the chief medium of his journalistic efforts on behalf of the American colonies. Not one of the contributions bore Franklin's name. Most were letters signed with pseudonyms, in the fashion of that century. Many were hoaxes, and Verner W. Crane, an authority on Franklin's propaganda, believes that H. S. Woodfall "more than once connived with his friend Franklin" in perpetrating them.[3]

On Thursday, April 16, 1747, one day after the *General Advertiser* published the speech of Polly Baker, two tri-weekly papers picked it up. One was the *St. James's Evening Post,* the other the *London Evening-Post.*[4] The "evening posts" were usually published on Tuesdays, Thursdays, and Saturdays, in time to catch the night mail for inland cities.[5]

Two more days passed, and on Saturday, April 18, the day before Easter, the London weeklies went into action. The speech showed up in the *Old England: or, The Broad-bottom Journal* and in the *Westminster Journal. Or, New*

3. For a sketch of Egelsham, see John Nichols, *Literary Anecdotes of the Eighteenth Century* (London, 1812), II, 702. Henry Woodfall, Jr., seems to have acquired stock in the paper in 1736 or 1737; "P. T. P.," in *Notes and Queries,* 1st ser., 12 (1855), 217. On the Franklin-Woodfall collaboration, see Verner W. Crane, ed., *Benjamin Franklin's Letters to the Press, 1758-1775* (Chapel Hill, 1950), xvi, 55, xxv-xxvi, 123n, 160, 237, 285.

4. For more about these and other publications of Polly's speech, see Bibliography, Part I, Chronological List of Printed Texts of Polly Baker's Speech, below, pp. 168-77.

5. The *Whitehall Evening-Post* for April and May does not contain the piece. The April issues of the *General Evening Post* have not been found. The semi-weekly *London Gazette* did not reprint Polly's speech.

Weekly Miscellany.[6] The weekly "journals," unlike the tri-weekly "evening posts" and the daily "advertisers," usually devoted page one to a long essay of some sort—political, religious, or otherwise. They filled the second, third, and fourth pages with news items and advertisements, including ads for patent medicines with infallible power to cure venereal diseases, seminal weaknesses, impotency in man, and barrenness in women. *Old England* placed Polly Baker at the end of the news items, not far from these advertisements, almost as if to invoke her as an endorser of "Superlative Enlivening Drops," which *"in a few Days render both Sexes Prolifick in a most wonderful Manner."*[7]

Easter came and went, and on Monday the 20th, a morning tri-weekly named the *Penny London Post, or, the Morning Advertiser,* belatedly echoed the heart-rending plea. And by this time the warmth of Polly's defense was radiating into other parts of the British Isles. A copy of the *General Advertiser* traveled eastward and reached Canterbury in time to squeeze Polly into the Saturday, April 18, issue of the *Kentish Post; or, The Canterbury News Letter.* A copy of the *London Evening-Post,* leaving London in a mailbag on the evening of Thursday the 16th, bounced westward over rough roads to Bath and reached an ingenious printer named Thomas Boddely, who thought well enough of Polly's words to reproduce them on Monday the 20th in his excellent weekly paper, the *Bath Journal.* The American heroine also pounded northward on the turnpike

6. The other London weeklies, *Read's Weekly Journal; Or, British Gazetteer;* and the *Country Journal; Or, The Craftsman,* have not been found. The *Anatomist,* presumably a weekly, appears in a list of London papers on the title page of the *Gentleman's Magazine* for April 1747, but copies apparently have not been preserved.

7. *Old England,* April 18, 1747.

to Northampton, in the center of England, where she spoke defiantly from the columns of Monday's *Northampton Mercury*. By Saturday the 25th, she had sped over land and sea and was haranguing the Irish from a Dublin newspaper with the interesting name of *Pue's Occurrences,* printed by Richard Pue at Dick's Coffee House in Skinner-Row. On or about April 27, back in England again, she bobbed up in the *Chester Courant.*[8]

It is impossible to say how many times this pattern repeated itself. Roughly thirty-five newspapers, most of them weeklies, were then being published in the provincial cities of England, plus perhaps seven in Ireland and two in Scotland—a total of about forty-four sheets in the British Isles outside London.[9] Copies of these papers for April 1747 are hard to find. Of the forty-four, only six are preserved in the British Museum and the Library of Congress. Five of these contain the speech of Polly Baker. Of those inaccessible, one can only assume that many printed Polly's plea.

If the newspapers left any English readers unconscious of Miss Baker's eloquence, the monthly magazines soon rushed in to make up the deficiency. Magazines were still in their infancy in 1747, but it was a most vigorous infancy. The *Gentleman's Magazine,* sixteen years old at the time, was the first publication to call itself a magazine. The term was used in the sense of a storehouse or collection. Month-

8. Although the *Courant* is unavailable, its version of the speech was reprinted in *The Chester Miscellany, Being a Collection of Several Pieces Both in Prose and Verse Which Were in the Chester Courant from January 1745-May 1750* (Chester, 1750), 223-26.

9. This estimate is based on the lists of newspapers in Bateson, ed., *Cambridge Bibliography of English Literature,* II, 720-36, and on the list printed each month on the title page of the *Gentleman's Magazine;* the list for April 1747 indicates that five English papers were being received which are not listed in the *Cambridge Bibliography.*

lies of a miscellaneous nature had been tried before in England, even as early as 1681 and 1692, but when the blue-covered *Gentleman's Magazine* first came off the press in 1731, the publishing world knew that it had been set afire.[10] As Samuel Johnson wrote twenty-three years later, the *Gentleman's* became "one of the most successful and lucrative pamphlets which literary history has upon record."[11] Johnson knew the *Gentleman's*—as a hungry young man he had been hired to help run the magazine.

The founder of the *Gentleman's Magazine,* who had employed Johnson and was still its publisher in 1747, was Edward Cave, a tall, heavy man who possessed two or three chins, a languid and discourteous manner, and a formidable case of gout. More important, he had an enterprising spirit and a bloodhound's nose for what would interest the reading public.[12] This sense of popular taste was to be evident in April 1751 when he printed the first edition of a small book which created a great stir—Benjamin Franklin's *Experiments and Observations on Electricity, made at Philadelphia in America.*

Sharing Franklin's eighteenth-century fondness for pen names, Cave published the *Gentleman's Magazine* under the rather comprehensive name "Sylvanus Urban." His periodical and its many imitators opened a rich variety of

10. For the *Gentleman's Magazine*'s predecessors and a discussion of the first twenty-three years of the magazine's existence, see "The Autobiography of Sylvanus Urban," *Gentleman's Magazine,* Vols. 201-202, July 1856-April 1857.

11. [Samuel Johnson], "An Account of the Life of the Late Mr Edward Cave," *Gentleman's Magazine,* 24 (1754), 57.

12. For biographical information on Cave, see *ibid.;* "The Autobiography of Sylvanus Urban," *Gentleman's Magazine,* espec. 201 (1856), 5, and 202 (1857), 385-87; and John Westby-Gibson's sketch of "Cave, Edward, 1691-1754" in the *Dictionary of National Biography,* IX, 338-40.

new ideas and new information to the reading public. When Cave founded the *Gentleman's,* he devoted a large part of the magazine to condensations of the essays in weekly journals, giving proper credit in each instance. To express his central purpose, he adopted the motto "E Pluribus Unum." (Later in the century the motto found its way onto the national seal of the United States—probably at the suggestion of Benjamin Franklin, who was a faithful reader of the *Gentleman's.*)[13]

Someone has called the *Gentleman's Magazine* "the fruitful mother of a thousand more,"[14] for there was scarcely a magazine during the rest of that century, either in Britain or America, which did not use it as a model. That other fruitful mother, Polly Baker, could not have asked for a better vehicle for conveying her sentiments to the world. Appropriately, when the *Gentleman's Magazine* for April 1747 came out at the end of April or the beginning of May, Polly Baker was there.[15]

Cave's most successful imitator and competitor was the *London Magazine.* Founded in 1732, the year after the *Gentleman's,* it made a gallant effort to surpass its prototype in the affections of the readers. Their fiercest rivalry came in the 1730's, but in 1747 they were still making the following claims: *Gentleman's Magazine*—"More in Quantity and greater Variety than any Book of the Kind and Price"; *London Magazine*—"Greater Variety, and more in Quantity, than any Monthly Book of the same Price." Both charged

13. Monroe E. Deutsch, "Our National Motto," *Pacific Spectator,* 9 (1955), 120-25.

14. Quoted from an unnamed source by Isaiah Thomas, *The History of Printing in America* (Worcester, Mass., 1810), II, 401n.

15. *Gentleman's Magazine,* 17 (1747), 175-76.

six shillings a copy.[16]   The *London Magazine,* trying to
live up to its boast, certainly could not afford to exclude
Polly Baker from its April issue.   There are signs, however,
that it came perilously close to doing so and finally inserted
the speech in haste at the last minute, snatching out the
customary list of new books and bankruptcies to make
room.[17]   At least, the April books and bankruptcies were
missing, and they showed up belatedly in the May issue,
where they occupied an amount of space exactly equal to
the speech.   Perhaps the *London Magazine* had learned by
the grapevine that Mr. Cave was printing Polly's words.

The only other monthly magazine published in London
was the *British Magazine,* which was then only in its second
year and sold at the more modest price of four shillings.   It
too printed Miss Baker's oration.[18]   Her language in the
London and *British* magazines is so nearly identical with
that of the *General Advertiser* that it is highly likely they
copied it directly from Woodfall's paper.

Cave had imitators in Scotland and Ireland, too.   At
Edinburgh, the *Scots Magazine,* founded in 1739, had a loyal
group of followers.   When the issue of April 1747 came out,
Polly was present.[19]   At Dublin, another *London Magazine,*
which librarians sometimes call "Exshaw's Magazine" because it was managed by two men named Exshaw, had be-

16. For the struggle between the magazines, see C. L. Carlson, *The First
Magazine* (Providence, 1938), 59-82.   The rival claims are taken from the title
pages of the April 1747 issues.   The selling price is given in the advertisements
placed by the two magazines in the *Daily Advertiser* of May 1, 1747.

17. *London Magazine,* 16 (1747), 178-79.

18. *British Magazine,* 2 (1747), 154-56.   This periodical, printed for C.
Corbett, at Addison's Head, in Fleet Street, should not be confused with the
British Magazine: or, the London and Edinburgh Intelligencer, which was pub-
lished at Edinburgh.

19. *Scots Magazine,* 9 (1747), 177-78.

gun publication in 1742 and every month was reprinting bodily most of the contents of the *London Magazine* of London. One of the items it lifted for its April 1747 issue was the speech of Polly Baker.[20]

That made five April magazines for Polly—the *Gentleman's,* the *London,* the *British,* the *Scots,* and "Exshaw's." In fact, there seem to have been only two monthly magazines in the British Isles that did not print the speech. These two, each only four months old at the time, were the *Newcastle General Magazine* and a second *British Magazine* brought out at Edinburgh.[21]

Scholars for a long time have mistakenly believed that Edward Cave was the first Englishman to publish the words of Polly Baker. Actually, Cave's text closely resembles that of the *General Advertiser* of April 15 and could easily have been copied from it. Nevertheless, some very strange things happened to her speech in Cave's hands.

20. *London Magazine* (Dublin), April 1747 (no volume number given), 172-73. This periodical was printed "for Edward and John Exshaw."

21. The seven periodicals named in this paragraph are the only British monthly magazines listed in the *Cambridge Bibliography* as extant in April 1747.

CHAPTER *Three*

Polly Bears Fifteen More Children—Or Does She?

WHEN Edward Cave reprinted the speech of Miss Polly Baker he was not content to serve it plain. He supplied some added attractions. It is just possible that Samuel Johnson, who was then thirty-eight, helped in this, for Johnson was still working for Cave on a part-time basis, according to John Nichols, who printed the *Gentleman's Magazine* later in the century. Nichols wrote concerning Johnson: "In 1747 he occasionally afforded his powerful assistance to the Magazine; and though many entire pieces cannot be ascertained to have come from his pen, he was frequently, if not constantly, employed to superintend the materials of the Magazine."[1]

The most important change had to do with Polly's married life. The newspapers had reported that her speech "influenced the Court to dispense with her Punishment, and induced one of her Judges to marry her the next Day." The

1. John Nichols, *The Rise and Progress of the Gentleman's Magazine* (London, 1821), xlii-xliii.

Gentleman's Magazine placed a comma after "Day" and added the words, *"by whom she has had fifteen Children."*

The newspaper account of Polly's trial had been somewhat vague concerning where and when it had taken place. As for the "where," the papers had quaintly said, "at Connecticut near Boston in New-England." As for the "when," they had given no clue at all. The announcement in the *Gentleman's Magazine* that she had become the mother of fifteen legitimate children after her marriage was startling, for it seemed to show that the trial was not a recent event.

This made twenty offspring for Polly, five before marriage and fifteen after. If the fertile Polly, in producing her fifteen lawful babies, had averaged one every two years, the trial must have taken place thirty years before publication of the speech—or in 1717. Even if she had performed a more astonishing feat of fertility, say a baby a year, it would have taken fifteen years, and this would place the courtroom scene in the year 1732. True, she could have done it faster if she had come from a family like the one mentioned in the *Gentleman's Magazine* of August 1731: "A Sadler's Wife was brought to Bed at *Perpignan, Aug.* 10. of five Girls; a Fortnight before her Sister lay in of 5 Boys, 4 of which are still living; their Mother, who had 15 Children, brought 12 of them into the World at three lyings in."[2] She could have made even better time if she had happened to be the woman who, according to a "we hear" item in Benjamin Franklin's *Pennsylvania Gazette* of November 24, 1738, gave birth to octuplets—seven girls and one boy—all living. Franklin credited this item to the *London Magazine* of August 1738, but it does not seem to be there. In any case,

2. *Gentleman's Magazine*, 1 (1731), 358.

these events were supposed to have occurred in Europe, not America. And assuming that Polly was not *that* fertile, a reader of the *Gentleman's Magazine* might justifiably have wondered why there had been such a long delay in reporting the news of the trial.

We cannot be certain that Edward Cave or his staff originated the line about the fifteen children. He may have picked it up from some source which has not been found. But it was not in any of the numerous April newspapers cited. It does not appear in the *British Magazine* or the *London Magazine* or the other *London Magazine* published by the Exshaws in Dublin. It does appear, however, in the account in the *Scots Magazine* at Edinburgh, and because of this and other textual similarities one must assume that the *Scots* copied the speech from the *Gentleman's*. Though both periodicals printed the piece in their issues of April 1747, there seems to be no doubt that the *Scots* went to press later than its counterparts in London and could have received the *Gentleman's* in time.[3]

But the most curious fact about the fifteen children is not that the magazines disagreed over their existence, but that the *Gentleman's Magazine* itself vacillated. The words *"by whom she has had fifteen Children"* appear in the April 1747 *Gentleman's Magazine* as found in the Boston Public Library, the Boston Athenaeum, the Massachusetts Historical Society, the American Antiquarian Society, the Maryland Historical Society, the American Philosophical Society, and the Bibliothèque Nationale. They also appear in the

3. The text of Polly's speech in the *Scots* followed that of the *Gentleman's* not only in the matter of the fifteen children but also in a few other details in which the *Gentleman's* differed from the *General Advertiser*.

two copies in the British Museum, the two copies in Bodleian Library, the two copies at the University of Chicago, the two copies at the Library Company of Philadelphia, and all three of the copies at Yale University.

On the other hand, the words *"by whom she has had fifteen Children"* do not appear in the April 1747 issue in the Library of Congress, or in the New York Public Library, or at Harvard University. Except for this one difference, the account is the same in all the libraries. Even the words and letters are spaced identically, with identical peculiarities of typography.[4] It is clear that the *Gentleman's Magazine* changed its mind during the process of printing the April issue.

Apparently Polly's fifteen children were originally present and then deleted. The evidence is perhaps not conclusive. The type seems to be slightly more battered in the versions without the seven words than in some of those that contain the statement about the children. Also, in the "fifteen children" version the two columns of type on the page are exactly the same length, but in the other version the columns are of uneven length—a fact which could be attributed to the removal of one line of type.

Why would someone on the mighty *Gentleman's Magazine*—presumably the editor, Edward Cave—remove a brief and amusing line after the edition had gone to press? Perhaps he belatedly realized that the added detail would strain the credulity of the *Gentleman's* readers, or, even more likely, he may have objected to the pushing of Polly's trial into the remote past by the advent of a large family. It would have been a routine matter for the printer to pluck out the

4. *Gentleman's Magazine*, 17 (1747), 175.

seven words, substitute a period for a comma, shove up tight the fifteen lines which remained in the column beneath the deletion, and drop a metal slug the size of the deleted line into the gap at the bottom of the column.

In distant Edinburgh, the copy of the *Gentleman's Magazine* that was delivered to the office of the *Scots Magazine* contained the version which had been printed before Polly's fifteen lawful offspring were exterminated. And in the distant twentieth century, most of the copies surviving in English and American libraries are of the same ilk. But through an odd circumstance, the copies preserved in America's three largest libraries depict a Polly Baker with only five children—not fifteen—clinging to her apron.

The *Gentleman's Magazine* also embellished Polly's speech with a scholarly footnote which linked her dilemma, somewhat tenuously, with John Milton, Joseph Addison, and Adam and Eve. Inevitably, we must wonder whether such a feat was the work of Samuel Johnson, then stuffed with learning and on the threshold of his fame.

Eighty years earlier, in 1667, Milton had published *Paradise Lost*. He was a powerful enemy of celibacy and often thundered against it. In Book IV of *Paradise Lost* there is a scene in which Adam and Eve retire for the night in their "inmost bower," and Milton exclaims:

> Our Maker bids increase; who bids abstain
> But our destroyer, foe to God and Man?
> Hail wedded Love, mysterious law, true source
> Of human offspring . . . .[5]

5. James Holly Hanford, ed., *The Poems of John Milton*, 2nd edn. (New York, 1953), 303.

In 1713, Joseph Addison's poetic tragedy *Cato* was first performed. Act V of this play opens with Cato sitting alone in a thoughtful posture. In his hand is a book by Plato on the immortality of the soul. On the table beside him is a drawn sword. He begins speaking:

> It must be so—Plato, thou reason'st well!—
> Else whence this pleasing hope, this fond desire,
> This longing after immortality?
> Or whence this secret dread, and inward horror,
> Of falling into nought?[6]

Cato argues with himself about immortality, first one way, then the other, and finally cries that he is weary of conjectures—"this must end 'em"—and lays his hand on the sword.

It remained for the *Gentleman's Magazine* to combine these two themes by Milton and Addison. In the issue of January 1747 was a piece of verse signed *Horatio* and entitled "The Maid's Soliloquy. Act V. Scene I. *of* Cato *Imitated.*" Under the title was a stage direction:

> *The Maid alone, with* Milton *in her hand, open*
> *at this celebrated Passage.*

> *—Hail wedded love! mysterious law!—&c.*
> *Our maker bids—Increase,—who bids abstain,*
> *But our destroyer, foe to God and man!*

The maid, reflecting on Milton's poem, now begins her soliloquy:

6. George H. Nettleton and Arthur E. Case, eds., *British Dramatists from Dryden to Sheridan* (Boston, 1939), 500.

It must be so—*Milton* thou reason'st well,
Else why this pleasing hope, this fond desire,
This longing after something unpossess'd;
Or whence this secret dread, and inward horror,
Of dying unespous'd?[7]

The maid argues with herself over whether to marry and finally says she is weary of these doubts—"the priest shall end them."

It was three months later, in the April issue, that the magazine printed the speech of Polly Baker, who invoked in her defense the first command of nature and of nature's God—increase and multiply. At one point Miss Baker declared, "I must be stupefied to the last degree, not to prefer the honourable state of wedlock, to the condition I have lived in."[8] Before the word "wedlock" the *Gentleman's Magazine* placed an asterisk. At the bottom of the column was this footnote: "See Maid's Soliloquy, *Jan. Mag. p.* 42." Thus Edward Cave—or someone working for him —placed Polly in high company.

But Cave did not stop there. In the same issue, the magazine expressed an editorial opinion about her personal appearance. Nineteen pages beyond the text of Polly's speech appeared the following stanza:

An EPIGRAM.

The vainly anxious *Myra* leaves
    To passive judges her complaints:
Her cause wou'd awe them, were they knaves;
    Her eyes wou'd bribe them, were they saints.

7. *Gentleman's Magazine,* 17 (1747), 42.
8. *Ibid.,* 175.

And immediately below this was a note that said: *"This may suit the beautiful* Polly Baker."[9]

At Edinburgh, the *Scots Magazine* printed the same poem and noted that it was "Applicable to Polly Baker."[10] And at Dublin, the Irish *London Magazine* also copied the poem and linked Myra with "the beautiful Polly Baker" in the same terms that the *Gentleman's Magazine* had used.[11] Even though the Messrs. Exshaw evidently lifted Polly's speech from the *London Magazine* of London in accordance with their custom, they clearly went over to the opposition in order to get on the bandwagon for accolades to Polly.

Though neither Cave nor the Exshaws knew it, the bandwagon was beginning a long ride, during which it would pick up a surprising assortment of passengers.

9. *Ibid.*, 194.
10. *Scots Magazine*, 9 (1747), 168.
11. *London Magazine* of Dublin ("Exshaw's Magazine"), April 1747 (no volume number), 182.

CHAPTER *Four*

Polly and the Chief Justice of Massachusetts

MISS Polly Baker, having made a triumphal British tour, now set sail for America. That is, a ship bearing copies of periodicals containing her speech left England in May 1747 and headed out across the broad Atlantic for Boston.

As Polly sailed westward, readers in England debated whether Polly Baker was a real person. Some suspected a hoax; others accepted the speech as an authentic news item. The *Northampton Mercury* on May 11, three weeks after giving Polly's words, printed an earnest letter entitled *"An Answer to* Polly Baker's *Speech."* The unidentified author gave nine reasons why the Divine Being forbids the two sexes of the human species to have libertine communication. For example, persons who so indulged "would be taken off from needful or profitable Employments by the Pursuit of their Pleasures"; they would be in danger of catching a "bad Distemper"; they would be often tempted to destroy their babies; and they either would be likely to become unvirtuous husbands and wives or would not marry at all, having already satisfied the urges of nature. The letter writer declared of Polly, "If any should say, as she does, that they have perform'd their Duty to the Publick, because they have produc'd Children; I reply, that they neither perform it to the Publick, nor to their Children: For it is not the Increase of the Species, but the furnishing the Society with useful Members, that is a Benefit to the Community." The writer aimed a formidable blow at Polly's contention that the Divine Being, having assisted in the production of her children, seemed not to have disapproved of her conduct. How little there is in this contention, said Polly's critic, "will appear by considering, that if she will now commit Adultery, he may equally concur to produce the Children that may be born of it, and yet sure she will not say that is any Proof of his not disliking it. Which Argument might even be carried farther, but I care not to pollute my Thoughts with it."[1]

At the end of May, before Polly's ship reached midocean, Edward Cave's magazine printed a remarkable communication which seemed to settle the controversy over the genuineness of Polly's speech. The table of contents of the *Gentleman's Magazine* for May 1747 contained the line, "Story of *Polly Baker* no fiction." Readers who turned to the appropriate page found a letter signed "William Smith." The letter began by referring to the footnote in the April issue which had described Polly as beautiful. The entire letter follows:

1. *Northampton Mercury*, May 11, 1747, 4.

Polly and the Chief Justice

Mr URBAN,

The note to the Epigram on *Mira*, p. 194, was very aptly added, for when I was in *New England*, in the year 1745, I had the pleasure of seeing the celebrated *Polly Baker*, who was then, though near 60 years of age, a comely woman, and the wife of *Paul Dudley*, Esq; of *Roxbury*, about two miles from *Boston*, who marry'd her, as it is mentioned in the papers, and had 15 children by her. I send you this information, because it has been insinuated, that the speech publish'd in her name, was entirely fictitious; that it could not be the speech of any woman (in which many females for different reasons concur) but was entirely the invention of some Templer or Garretteer.

It must be noted that it is the custom in this country, for young persons between whom there is a courtship, or treaty of marriage, to lye together, the woman having her petticoats on, and the man his breeches, and afterwards, if they do not fall out, they confess the covenant at church, in the midst of the congregation, and to the minister, who declares the marriage legal; and if any thing criminal has been acted, orders a punishment accordingly, sometimes of forty stripes save one.

I am, Sir, Yours, &c,
WILLIAM SMITH.[2]

This was sensational news, for Paul Dudley was the chief justice of Massachusetts. Then nearly seventy-two years old, he was one of the most eminent men in New England. Both his father Joseph Dudley and his grandfather Thomas Dudley had been Massachusetts governors.

2. *Gentleman's Magazine*, 17 (1747), 211.

Paul Dudley was born in 1675. At the age of ten he entered Harvard, and was graduated at fourteen, adding a master's degree at seventeen. About five years later he made the long voyage to England and studied law at the Inner Temple. When he returned, he seems to have been the only professionally trained lawyer in Massachusetts. He became attorney general in 1702 when his father became governor.[3] While attorney general he was also one of the justices of the peace for Suffolk County, and in that capacity he sometimes served on the panel of justices when parents of bastard children were tried for fornication.[4] Appointed to the Superior Court in 1718, he was elevated to the chief justiceship in 1745. He shared the strong religious feelings of his day, especially against what he called the "damnable Heresies" and "abominable Superstitions" of the Church of Rome.[5] He also had a strong intellectual curiosity and could put the coveted initials F. R. S. (Fellow of the Royal Society) after his name, an honor that came to few Americans.

After the publication of the William Smith letter, Englishmen who had challenged the authenticity of Polly Baker in coffeehouse conversations or family arguments must have retired in disorder.

Another month passed. During June, the ship bearing Polly's speech continued to crawl over the face of the Atlantic, subject to the vagaries of the winds. The periodicals

3. For an excellent biographical sketch, see Clifford K. Shipton, *Sibley's Harvard Graduates* (Cambridge, Mass., 1933), IV, 42-54.
4. Entries for July 6 and 27, 1702, Records of the Court of General Sessions of the Peace, Beginning July 1702, Ending July 1712 (Suffolk County Courthouse, Boston).
5. Dudley's will, dated Jan. 1, 1750, quoted in appendix to John Barnard, *A Proof of Jesus Christ's, Being the Promised Messiah* (Boston, 1756).

on board still had not reached their destination when another bombshell exploded in London. The *Gentleman's Magazine* for June 1747 printed a letter signed "L. Americanus," which went as follows:

June 1, 1747

Mr URBAN,

The Author of the letter in your Magazine for *May,* sign'd *William Smith,* is egregiously imposed upon; for 'tis well known, that *Paul Dudley,* Esq; never acted in any judicial capacity in *Connecticut,* but is chief justice of the province where he has always resided, and has been long married to a daughter of the late Gov. WINTHROP, by whom he never had any children.

As they are of very good families, and he is one of the first rank in the country, 'tis pity their names should be ignorantly or wantonly used in support of a fictitious speech.

The scurrilous description of the customs of young persons, if in use at all, is among the very lowest sort of people only.

Yours, &c. L. AMERICANUS.[6]

By this time, English readers of the *Gentleman's Magazine* must have felt a little dizzy. But Paul Dudley and other New Englanders were comfortably unaware of the conflicting statements of "William Smith" and "L. Americanus." The text of the speech itself, however, drew ever nearer to American shores. One day around the middle of July, the April periodicals sailed into Boston Bay, and soon thereafter the American press began reporting the news about Polly's trial.

6. *Gentleman's Magazine,* 17 (1747), 295.

A dozen weekly newspapers served the people of the thirteen colonies in that summer of 1747. There were four at Boston, three at New York, two at Philadelphia, and one each at Annapolis, Williamsburg, and Charleston.[7] There were not yet any dailies in America. The weekly sheets modeled themselves after the bigger and more prosperous London newspapers, and they depended upon the British journals and magazines for much of their contents.

Of the four Boston newspapers, the only one to carry the speech was the *Boston Weekly Post-Boy,* a two-page newspaper, which on Monday, July 20, published the speech at the top of its first page. It preceded the piece with a notice that *"the following remarkable Speech is printed both in the* London *and* Gentleman's Magazines *for the Month of* April *last; as also in several of the* London & *other* British *late News Papers."* Next came the usual paragraph giving the circumstances of the trial. The words "Connecticut near Boston in New-England" were reduced to "Con--ct-cut, *N.E."* Nothing was said about the fifteen children after marriage. The printer made a few changes in Polly's language, so that the text is not identical with that of any British periodical. Immediately following the speech was a brief item, credited to the *London Magazine* for April, to the effect that in Yorkshire lived two brothers named Stonecliff who together weighed 980 pounds.

We have no record of Paul Dudley's reaction to the account of Polly's trial, but we may assume that the piece was read with interest and perhaps even with surprise in the Province of Massachusetts-Bay, and also in nearby "Con--ct-cut" where the proceedings reportedly had taken place.

---

7. Charles Evans, *American Bibliography* (Chicago, 1903), I, 440-41.

The *Boston Weekly Post-Boy* was printed "for E. Huske, Post-master," and Mr. Huske no doubt was in a position to see that his paper was speedily delivered to outlying districts of New England. Connecticut had no newspapers of its own to reprint Polly's speech, but copies of the Boston paper soon reached New York.

On Monday, August 3, 1747, Polly's argument became front-page news in the *New-York Gazette, Revived in the Weekly Post-Boy,* a small four-page paper printed by James Parker, whose silent partner in the firm was Benjamin Franklin of Philadelphia. On the same day, the speech occupied the whole front page of the *New-York Weekly Journal,* another small four-page sheet *"Printed by the Widow* Cathrine Zenger." Her late husband John Peter Zenger had been the defendant in a famous trial for seditious libel a dozen years earlier, and his acquittal had been hailed as a great victory for freedom of the press.[8]

These two New York weeklies unquestionably copied the speech of Polly Baker from the *Boston Weekly Post-Boy.* They referred to the British printings in the same words the Boston paper had used. They conformed closely to the Boston text. And immediately after the speech they did not neglect to describe the Stoneclift brothers whose combined weight was 980 pounds.

In Philadelphia, neither Franklin's *Pennsylvania Gazette* nor its rival, the *Pennsylvania Weekly Journal,* picked up the speech of Polly Baker. But in Annapolis, Maryland,

8. Whitfield J. Bell, Jr., associate editor of *The Papers of Benjamin Franklin,* called my attention to the speech in the New York weeklies. The other New York paper, the *Evening Post,* does not contain Polly's speech. For Franklin's partnership with Parker, see Carl Van Doren, *Benjamin Franklin* (New York, 1938), 120, 122; George Simpson Eddy, ed., *Account Books Kept by Benjamin Franklin* (New York, 1929), II, 95-97.

one of the most perplexing episodes in Polly's entire history now took place.

On Tuesday, August 11, 1747, Jonas Green, the fun-loving printer of the *Maryland Gazette,* devoted his front page to Polly Baker. "The following very famous SPEECH has been published in the *London* and *Gentleman's Magazines* for *April* past, as well as in some other *British* Papers; but was there printed incorrectly, which I suppose was occasioned by the Mutilation it suffer'd, in passing through the Hands of Transcribers before it reach'd the Press in *London*: And happening to have a correct Copy of it by me, I cannot think it amiss to give it my Readers, not doubting it's favourable Reception."[9]

Jonas Green did not tell his readers where he got the correct copy which he just happened to have by him. Before coming to Annapolis in 1738, he had worked as a printer in two other towns. The first was Boston, where he was born in 1712. The second was Philadelphia, where he lived for a few years in the late 1730's and worked for both Benjamin Franklin and Andrew Bradford, rival printers of that city.[10] Green is not well-known today, but he was a prominent figure in the Maryland capital for nearly thirty years until his death in 1767, serving as public printer of the province, postmaster, alderman, vestryman, and in other capacities. He proudly wore the title "Poet, Printer, Punster, Purveyor and Punchmaker general" in a convivial group called the Tuesday Club of Annapolis, which was fond of mock trials and humorous orations, but whose vo-

9. Mr. Bell also called the *Maryland Gazette* printing to my attention.
10. Lawrence C. Wroth, *A History of Printing in Colonial Maryland, 1686-1776* (Baltimore, 1922), 75-76; Isaiah Thomas, *The History of Printing in America,* 2nd edn. (Albany, 1874), I, 128.

luminous minutes do not mention Polly Baker.[11] Green's
fellow members recorded a story, which may have been true
or may have been a good-natured spoof, to the effect that
they sent one of his poems to a London friend in 1751 with
instructions to have it inserted in some English magazine.
According to this account, Edward Cave refused to print it
in the *Gentleman's Magazine,* and the publisher of the
Universal Magazine distorted his face into "a very con-
temptuous leer" and told the emissary that the author of the
poem was a fool.[12]

Polly's speech as it appeared in Green's *Maryland Gazette* differed from the British versions in several minor
ways and one major way. The most important difference
took the form of a mysterious insertion just after Polly's plea
to her hearers not to make laws which turn natural and
useful actions into crimes. "Reflect a little," the insertion
warned, "on the horrid Consequences of this Law in particular: What Numbers of procur'd Abortions! and how
many distress'd Mothers have been driven, by the Terror of
Punishment and public Shame, to imbrue, contrary to
Nature, their own trembling Hands in the Blood of their
helpless Offspring! Nature would have induc'd them to
nurse it up with a Parent's Fondness. 'Tis the Law therefore, 'tis the Law itself that is guilty of all these Barbarities
and Murders. Repeal it then, Gentlemen; let it be expung'd
for ever from your Books."[13]

11. The manuscript minutes of the Tuesday Club for 1745-1755 are in the
Maryland Historical Society, Baltimore, and those for 1755-1756 are in the
Library of Congress.

12. Joseph Towne Wheeler, "Reading and Other Recreations of Marylanders,
1700-1776," *Maryland Historical Magazine,* 38 (1943), 54.

13. The newspaper provided a note indicating that Polly addressed all these
remarks to *"some Gentlemen of the Assembly, then in Court."* The passage
does not appear in any other known printing of Polly's speech.

By the end of August, we may assume, the William Smith letter in the May number of the *Gentleman's Magazine* had arrived in Boston and come to the attention of Paul Dudley and his lady. William Smith stated flatly that he had recently seen the celebrated Polly Baker, who was then, though nearly sixty years old, a comely woman and Dudley's wife.

Justice Dudley was not a man to take a tolerant view of such goings-on. After he died in January 1751, a Boston newspaper described his character thus: "As his Presence always commanded Respect, so it might justly be said of him that he scatter'd Iniquity with his Eyes, which struck with Awe the most daring Offenders." In addition he had a great "abhorrence of Vice." Dudley, this account went on, possessed "quick Apprehension," "uncommon Strength of Memory," and "extensive Knowledge." He labored under "great Indispositions of Body," which were often heavy upon him while he attended the business of the court, and this perhaps was what caused his "Impatience" and his expressing himself "with some Appearance of Severity." But if the Justice thereby "gave any Disgust in public," he made full amends for it in private, for he was charming in conversation and "one of the most tender Husbands."[14]

This tender husband and scatterer of iniquity was prevented by three thousand miles of ocean from fixing his terrible eyes on Edward Cave; nevertheless it is entirely possible that he awed him. He may have denounced Cave in a letter and perhaps added a postscript defending the

14. Stephen Sewall, *The Character of the Late Honorable Judge Dudley, as it was inserted in the Boston-Newsletter, Feb. 7, 1751* (Boston, 1751), reprinted in Ebenezer Gay, *Natural Religion as Distinguished from Revealed* (Boston, 1759), appendix.

good name of Massachusetts in the matter of bundling. He may have threatened to sue for libel. He may have sued for libel. At any rate, the *Gentleman's Magazine,* after keeping a cautious silence on this subject for more than a year, finally made a groveling apology in the issue of July 1748:

WHEREAS, thro' the wicked contrivance of one *William Smith,* we unwarily publish'd in our Magazine for *May* 1747, a letter sign'd by him, which we are now fully sensible contains a most groundless, vile and injurious slander and imputation upon the Hon. *Paul Dudley,* Esq; his Majesty's chief justice of the province of the *Massachusetts Bay,* the principal province in *New England;* and his lady, a person of the most unblemish'd reputation, and remarkable during her whole life for her great modesty, virtue, and other amiable qualities: And whereas the said *William Smith* hath since absconded, so that he cannot lawfully be punish'd for his malicious and gross abuse, we being desirous that all possible reparation should be made in this case, do hereby publickly confess our great concern that we should suffer ourselves to be imposed on, and become the means of publishing so great a calumny, and ask pardon of Mr *Dudley* and his lady for the same.

And whereas the said letter also contains a base and scandalous aspersion upon the inhabitants of the aforesaid province, by representing their customs in points of marriage as extremely irregular and indecent, contrary to the truth and to the standing laws of that province, approved by the king in council, we ask pardon of the said province for having publish'd the same.[15]

15. *Gentleman's Magazine,* 18 (1748), 332.

This language strongly suggests that it was drafted by a lawyer. It could have been written by Dudley himself. Indeed, the apology is concerned only with the Dudleys' role in the Polly Baker case and, to a lesser extent, with bundling in Massachusetts. Although Cave humbly apologized to the chief justice and his wife, he did not retract Polly's speech or deny its authenticity.

The faithful readers of the *Gentleman's Magazine* must have speculated about Polly for a long time, but they got no further enlightenment from that magazine. As late as 1781, a subscriber, in a letter to the editor, recalled the publication of the speech "said to have been spoken by Mrs. P. Baker" and asked if any of the magazine's numerous correspondents could give information concerning its origin.[16] If anyone did, the magazine failed to print it.

A modern investigator, seeking to learn how the chief justice of Massachusetts was dragged into the affair, finds himself beset by inaccuracies on all sides. In the first place, Dudley never married anyone named Polly Baker. But when "L. Americanus" said that Dudley had married a daughter of Governor Winthrop he too was mistaken. The truth is that Dudley married Lucy Wainwright, of a highly respected family in Ipswich, Massachusetts. This took place in 1703, after Dudley had become a justice of the peace and attorney general. They were man and wife until his death in 1751. They did *not* have fifteen children, but on the other hand "L. Americanus" was incorrect when he said they never had any. They had six, all of whom died in infancy.[17]

16. *Ibid.*, 51 (1781), 367.
17. Shipton, *Sibley's Harvard Graduates*, IV, 44; and Barnard, *Proof of Jesus Christ*, preface.

It was true that Dudley had family connections with the Winthrops. His sister Ann Dudley married John Winthrop, great-grandson of the John Winthrop who was the original governor of Massachusetts Bay. His wife's sister Ann Wainwright married Adam Winthrop, another great-grandson of the original Governor John Winthrop and for many years a Suffolk County justice along with Paul Dudley. Besides, long before Paul Dudley was born, his uncle the Reverend Samuel Dudley married Mary Winthrop, who was indeed a daughter of the original Governor John Winthrop.[18]

Those marriages may have confused "L. Americanus." What confused William Smith, if that was really his name, may never come to light. Though he erred concerning the identity of Mrs. Paul Dudley, he seems to have been substantially correct about bundling—or, as he put it, the custom for young persons between whom there was a courtship to "lye together" with their garments on. This practice was found in both Connecticut and Massachusetts, and in fact was nearing its height at that very time. But colonial New England had no Dr. Kinsey, and not much is known about bundling. It seems clear that the custom, whatever it was, prevailed mainly among the humbler country people whose houses were cold in the New England winters. Persons of wealth and position, like Paul Dudley and perhaps "L. Americanus," looked upon bundling (if they heard of it at all) with disapproval and contempt. It was natural for them to resent publicity about it.[19]

18. Lawrence Shaw Mayo, *The Winthrop Family in America* (Boston, 1948), 24, 107, 140-41, 150, 152.
19. On bundling, see Henry Reed Stiles, *Bundling: Its Origin, Progress and Decline in America* (Albany, 1871), 108-9; Arthur W. Calhoun, *A Social*

Who was William Smith? Was he Edward Cave in disguise? At least one writer has thought so.[20] But why would Cave, in selecting a husband for Polly, hit upon so imposing a person as the chief justice of Massachusetts? It makes more sense to suppose that someone sent the letter to Cave and that he was over-eager to accept it as true.

Some real William Smiths existed, of course. One, an Anglican clergyman, was later to become a bitter enemy of Benjamin Franklin at Philadelphia; and another once published a newspaper at Freeport, Dominica, in association with Franklin, who invested in such enterprises in a number of cities, taking part of the profits.[21] But there is no reason to think that any real William Smith wrote the letter.

Whoever did write it may have combined his fun with a sizable amount of malice. The chief justice did not lack enemies. Paul Dudley and his father before him had been embroiled for half a century in personal and political feuds with other factions in Massachusetts. As a young attorney general, Paul was accused of accepting bribes. He was unpopular with the radicals of Boston and in 1722 was attacked in the *New-England Courant,* published by James Franklin with the help of his younger brother Ben.[22] This

---

History of the American Family (Cleveland, 1917), I, 129-30; George R. Stewart, *American Ways of Life* (Garden City, N.Y., 1954), 186. When William Smith wrote that ministers imposed punishments for fornication, "sometimes of forty stripes save one," he was on less solid ground than he was on bundling. Ministers could not inflict such penalties. In the criminal cases in the courts, the punishments rarely exceeded "10 stripes." For a discriminating account of secular and ecclesiastical authority, see Emil Oberholzer, Jr., *Delinquent Saints: Disciplinary Action in the Early Congregational Churches of Massachusetts* (New York, 1956).

20. Howard Payson Arnold, *Historic Side-lights* (New York, 1899), 147.
21. Van Doren, *Franklin,* 122, 193-94.
22. Shipton, *Sibley's Harvard Graduates,* IV, 45, 48-49.

was the year before Benjamin Franklin ran away from his Boston home and started life anew in Philadelphia.

The governor of Massachusetts in the 1730's, Jonathan Belcher, detested Dudley and referred to him in correspondence as "a prostitute to every thing that's mean and vile," "our Sarah," "the filthy slut," and "filthy baggage."[23] Could these epithets be allusions to some scandal in Dudley's life? Granted that he never married anyone named Polly Baker, was it nevertheless possible that in his twenties he had been the bachelor who originally got her with child, and that he later became the magistrate who was "advanc'd to Honour and Power in the Government, that punishes my Misfortunes with Stripes and Infamy"?[24]

Such speculation is made more tantalizing by a note which appeared at the end of one of the later reprintings of Polly's speech: "N. B. Another account says her name was Sarah Olitor."[25] Was this why Governor Belcher referred to Dudley as "our Sarah"? Perhaps the epithet was only Belcher's way of calling Dudley a scold. Possibly, it was an allusion to Sarah Millwood, the villainous prostitute of George Lillo's play, *The London Merchant,* which had been introduced at London in 1731.

At any rate, there appears to have been no scandal in Paul Dudley's life, and it is only fair to cite Clifford K. Shipton's estimate of the jurist: "Much has been quoted against the character of Paul Dudley, largely from preju-

---

23. *Ibid.,* 50. The letters containing these epithets were written in 1740; Massachusetts Historical Society, *Collections,* 6th ser., 7 (1894), 299, 260, 305, 310.

24. *General Advertiser,* April 15, 1747.

25. *American Museum* (Philadelphia), 1st edn., 1 (1787), 245. This mysterious Sarah will be discussed in a later chapter.

diced sources. . . . For thirty-three years as a judge he was noted among his contemporaries for honesty, courage, and ability."[26] The affair of Dudley's accuser, William Smith, remains one of the unsolved mysteries that cluster around Polly Baker.

26. Shipton, *Sibley's Harvard Graduates,* IV, 52.

CHAPTER *Five*

Polly and the English Deist

THE periodical press had made Polly Baker a familiar name. It remained for an English deist to make her a saint.

The deist's name was Peter Annet.[1] Like other deists, he believed in a religion of nature and reason, not of prayer and revelation. He rejected the authority of churches and clergy. He denied the performance of miracles and judged the Bible and all other books by the following criterion: "If a man tells me that he has crossed Westminster Bridge, the story may be true and deserves examination, though the Bridge is not quite finished; but if he says that he jumped the river, I know the story to be a lie and trouble myself no more about it."[2] Annet believed in God, but in a God that created the universe and its moral laws and then stood aside, leaving the universe to run of itself. He was outraged

1. Norman L. Torrey discusses Annet's philosophy in *Voltaire and the English Deists* (New Haven, 1930), 7-8, 174 ff.
2. Peter Annet, *A Collection of the Tracts of a Certain Free Enquirer, Noted by His Sufferings for His Opinions* (London? 1766?), 140, quoted by Leslie Stephen, *History of English Thought in the Eighteenth Century* (3rd edn., 1902, reprinted New York, 1927), I, 252. Stephen indicates that Annet wrote the passage in 1747.

by any man-made law which he considered to conflict with God's legislation.

Deism was an important movement in the religious and philosophical histories of England, France, and America. It was not an organized movement; it did not enroll large masses of people calling themselves deists. But it gradually infiltrated many minds and had a liberalizing effect on religion in general. Some of the greatest and most influential men of the eighteenth century were deists at heart, or nearly so. Deism became a significant part of the heritage with which the United States began its independent existence.[3]

In England, from the latter part of the seventeenth century to the middle years of the eighteenth, the torch of deism was carried by a series of able writers who waged fierce controversies with Christian theologians over the resurrection and other supernatural events of the Scriptures. By the time Polly Baker's speech was published in 1747 the deistical arguments had somewhat abated—but not for at least one of these writers, Peter Annet. Roughly, savagely, with grim humor and gusto he slammed away at the veracity and behavior of Biblical heroes, especially Paul, David, and Moses. Students of English thought have pointed out that Annet was the connecting link between the English deism of the early part of the eighteenth century and the more aggressive and outspoken deism of Thomas Paine and the revolutionary period.[4]

3. The standard study is H. M. Morais, *Deism in Eighteenth Century America* (New York, 1934).

4. Torrey, *Voltaire and the English Deists,* 175; Stephen, *English Thought in the Eighteenth Century,* I, 247.

SOCIAL BLISS

CONSIDERED:

In MARRIAGE and DIVORCE; COHABITING UNMARRIED, and PUBLIC WHORING.

CONTAINING

Things neceſſary to be known by all that ſeek mutual Felicity, and are ripe for the Enjoyment of it.

WITH

The SPEECH of Miſs POLLY BAKER; and Notes thereon.

——————Man when created,
At firſt alone, long wandered up and down,
Forlorn and ſilent as his Vaſſal Beaſt;
But when a Heav'n-born Maid to him appear'd,
Strange Paſſion fill'd his Eyes, and fir'd his Heart,
Unloos'd his Tongue, and his firſt Talk was Love.

OTWAY.

By GIDEON ARCHER. *P. Annet*

LONDON:

Printed for and ſold by R. ROSE, near St. *Paul's.*

M. DCC. XLIX.

(Price Two Shillings.)

SOCIAL BLISS CONSIDERED

Peter Annet's pamphlet appeared in 1749 under the pseudonym, "Gideon Archer."

Polly and the English Deist

In February 1749, a little less than two years after the British newspapers and magazines had printed the speech of Polly Baker, there was published in London a book called *Social Bliss Considered: In Marriage and Divorce; Cohabiting unmarried, and Public Whoring.* Beneath this title were the words, "Containing Things necessary to be known by all that seek mutual Felicity, and are ripe for the Enjoyment of it." The author was given as Gideon Archer, but this was a pseudonym. The real author was Peter Annet.[5]

In this book Annet argued strenuously in favor of wedlock, placing his views in opposition to the celibacy of St. Paul. He advocated divorce in case a union turned out unhappily. He advised young women to remain virgins until marriage, and young men to be moderate in their sex lives, but he urged parents to forgive the indiscretions of their children. He said public whoring should be allowed under proper regulations as a means of preventing "private whoring." *"Where there is no law, there is no transgression,"* he said. "Take away therefore the *law,* and you take away the *sin;* for 'tis none against *nature.* . . . These familiar social favours, which will always be wanted, sought

5. In their issues for February 1749, the *Gentleman's Magazine, London Magazine,* and *British Magazine* (London) listed this book by "Gideon Archer" among the new books published in that month. *Social Bliss Considered* was later reprinted in *A Collection of the Tracts of a Certain Free Enquirer, Noted by His Sufferings for His Opinions.* Although the title page bears no author, publisher, date, or place of publication, the "Certain Free Enquirer" is generally recognized as Peter Annet, who had been punished for publishing a weekly called the *Free Enquirer* in 1761. S. Austin Allibone, in *A Critical Dictionary of English Literature and British and American Authors Living and Deceased* (Philadelphia, 1870), I, 63, places the publication date at 1766 and accepts Annet as author. Torrey, *Voltaire and the English Deists,* 187, assigns authorship to Annet, and so does Leslie Stephen in his article on Annet in the *Dictionary of National Biography,* II, 9.

for, and granted, both are and may be done, without prejudice to *society*."[6]

Such ideas about laws and transgressions were not exclusive to Peter Annet; for example, in distant Boston, twenty-six years earlier, the *New-England Courant,* published by James and Benjamin Franklin, had printed a manuscript which it said was "found in the Street," and which contained these words: "Where there is no Law, there can be no Transgression."[7]

On the title page of Annet's book, beneath the title and subtitle already quoted, appeared the additional statement,

WITH

The SPEECH of Miss POLLY BAKER; and

Notes thereon.

Near the conclusion of the book, Annet quoted Polly's oration in full. He did not cite his source, but the text was substantially the same as that of the *General Advertiser* and the English magazines in 1747. It seems likely he took the speech from the *London Magazine.* He made no reference to the fifteen children who, according to some copies of the *Gentleman's Magazine,* had been born to Polly after her marriage.[8]

Instead of claiming flatly that the speech was "delivered" by her, Annet commented that it was *"said to be delivered by her."* Thus he covered himself against the possibility that Polly was not a historical fact. Yet he felt impatient toward those who disbelieved her account, for he wrote the following footnote: "This story is attested for truth, but

6. Peter Annet ("Gideon Archer"), *Social Bliss Considered* (London, 1749), 108.

7. *New-England Courant,* Feb. 4, 1723.

8. Annet, *Social Bliss Considered,* 99-105.

whether true or no, the reasons that follow are true; but many persons, in matters of belief, *strain at a gnat, and swallow a camel*: They cannot credit the truth of a story that has nothing improbable in it; but can credit stories reported by a credulous people to be done in distant ages, and in a strange country, which are impossible to nature."[9]

This was only the first of twenty-five footnotes—from "a" to "y"—in which Annet played a busy chorus in Polly's drama, commenting on her actions, supporting her arguments, and generally amplifying her plea into a full-blown diatribe against Christianity and the laws of man. Polly begins by announcing that she is "a poor unhappy woman, who have no money to fee lawyers to plead for me, being hard put to it to get a tolerable living." Annet begins with a broad application of her remark and a warning shake of his finger: "No penny, no *pater noster* whether in Law or Gospel, the poor could seldom have right by law, and formerly 'twas *impossible* for rich men to go to heaven by the gospel, when *Christ* and his ministers were poor; but if the case be the same now, *Christ* have mercy upon his ministers, for they are now rich."

Polly then says, "I have not the presumption to expect, that you may by any means be prevailed on to deviate in your sentence from the law in my favour." In reply Annet continues his own train of thought, citing chapter, if not verse: "Religious sinners have more assurance; they imagine, as they are taught, *Luke* xviii, that *importunity* will work upon their judge, and that therefore *they shall be heard for their much speaking*, . . . or, why do they pray so long, and often?"

9. *Ibid.*, 99.

Clearly, however, repetition is familiar to Annet. As Polly's plea continues, he restates her already eloquent defense in greater detail. Let Polly Baker and Peter Annet have the floor, quoting from her speech and his footnotes, for their litany reveals a characteristic to which we may attribute much of Polly's long life: her convenience to an age that thrived on questioning the order of man's world and God's universe.[10]

POLLY: . . . laws are sometimes unreasonable in themselves, and therefore repealed; and others bear too hard on the subject in particular circumstances, and therefore there is left a power somewhat to dispense with the execution of them. . . .

ANNET: And very reasonable it should be so, because circumstances so far alter the nature of things, that the same action may be good or evil, as it is differently circumstanced.

POLLY: Abstracted from the law I cannot conceive (may it please your Honours) what the nature of my offence is.

ANNET: 'Twould be very hard by the laws of reason and nature, without the arbitrary authority of law, to prove her a criminal, or offender. Can an inoffensive life offend God, that does not offend man?

. . . .

POLLY: . . . I must now complain of it, as unjust and unequal, that my betrayer and undoer . . . should be advanc'd to honour and power in the government, that punishes my misfortunes with stripes and infamy.

10. The language is unchanged except for rearrangement into dialogue form. Both Polly's quotations and Annet's footnotes are from Annet, *Social Bliss Considered,* 99-105.

ANNET: It must be confess'd, tho' 'tis disagreeable to be told, that people do not suffer for their *crimes,* but for their *weakness, ignorance* and *poverty*: For if two persons are guilty of the same action (as in this case) the impotent and poor suffer with scandal, while the powerful and opulent generally escape with impunity, and perhaps applause, tho' the poor may have necessity to plead in their favour; and this is naturally the case, when actions that are not criminal in themselves are so made by law; or actions criminal in reason and the nature of things, are by law or custom esteem'd just. Sometimes indeed men suffer for their riches, as when they fall into the hands of *high-way* robbers, or *high-church* robbers, as the inquisition in *Spain* and *Portugal,* where rich Heretics are *murdered* by the law of that church, that the church by law too may *rob* them and their families of all their wealth; and this law is *there* deemed *holy* and *just.*

POLLY: I shall be told, 'tis like, that were there no act of assembly in the case, the precepts of religion are violated by my transgressions.

ANNET: The precepts of any religion, which is not established on the foundations of *truth* and *honesty,* (and they are generally founded on somewhat else) are violated by truth and honesty. Religion, erected and established on these, is good; and such religion only. All other is knavery, and tyranny, and injurious to the natural rights of mankind. . . .

Polly concludes that she deserves a statue instead of a whipping, for she has obeyed God's command to increase and multiply. Annet is, by this time, almost reverent in his admiration as he intones his last footnote: "This speech is beyond all statues that can be erected to eternize her memory, which demonstrate her to have been a woman of excellent SENSE, VIRTUE AND HONOUR, maugre all that may be said to the contrary."

This man who wrote about Polly Baker in terms fit for a saint, or at least one of the blessed ones whose memory should be eternal, was in disgrace with the church for most of his life. Born in 1693, he was a school teacher as a young man but was fired in the early 1740's for publishing disrespectful comments on the writings of the Bishop of London and other leading churchmen. In 1761 he published anonymously a controversial book called *David, the History of the Man after God's Own Heart*. It was at about this time that Voltaire was starting his heaviest campaign against institutionalized Christianity. Voltaire, more brilliant and effective than any of the English deists, owed much to their writings and was himself basically a deist without calling himself one. He obtained a copy of Annet's anonymous book about David and adapted it into a drama, *Saül,* which he pretended was a translation from the English.[11]

In 1763, Annet, aged and feeble, was tried for attempting "to infuse and propagate irreligious and diabolical opinions in the minds of his majesty's subjects and to shake the foundations of the Christian religion and of the civil and ecclesiastical government established in this kingdom."[12] Possibly a random thought of Polly Baker flitted across his mind as he stood mute and offered no defense. He was found guilty and sent to the pillory, afterwards serving a year at hard labor. In six years he was dead.

11. Torrey, *Voltaire and the English Deists,* 8, 187-89.
12. Stephen, "Peter Annet," *Dictionary of National Biography,* II, 9.

Probably in 1766, though the date is not given, several of Annet's earlier writings were published in a book entitled *A Collection of the Tracts of a Certain Free Enquirer, Noted by His Sufferings for His Opinions*.[13] Among the tracts was *Social Bliss Considered,* and by this means the words of Polly Baker were circulated again to British readers. And so were Annet's twenty-five footnotes.

Not all deists would have been so deeply stirred by the speech as Peter Annet was. But his enthusiasm for it doubtless convinced at least some readers that Polly Baker, fact or fiction, was effective propaganda for deism.

13. See note 5, p. 51.

CHAPTER *Six*

Polly and the French Firebrands

A S the eighteenth century moved toward its cataclysmic final quarter, newspapers here and there kept Polly's speech alive. For example, in 1768 a translation appeared in the Swedish periodical *Posten* which took the story seriously and gave the *London Magazine* as the source.[1] On February 16, 1773, a paper in Salem, Massachusetts, the *Essex Gazette,* printed the speech beneath this communication: "Messieurs *Printers,* By inserting the following (tho' of an ancient date) you will doubtless oblige many of your readers, besides, your's, &c. *J. C.*" The text was quite close to that of the *Gentleman's Magazine.* A month and a half later—on April 1—the *Virginia Gazette* at Williamsburg published Polly's words with credit to the *Essex Gazette.*

But Polly's greatest popularity in the 1770's came in France. Her role as one of the oppressed who dared speak out, her appeal to the universal laws of nature and reason, and her defiant challenge to arbitrary prohibitions—all these suited the rising revolutionary spirit in that country. Her name was blazoned throughout the civilized world by a popular French historian, the Abbé Raynal.

1. Johansson, *Diderot,* 178n.

Guillaume-Thomas Raynal was an audacious little man with a commanding nose and an impressive gift of gab. Born in 1713, he began his career as a Jesuit priest; hence his title, "Abbé." When still a young man he parted with the Society of Jesus—some said because of his ambition—and found himself in Paris free from churchly discipline in 1747, the same year the British press was introducing the speech of Polly Baker. Raynal became a writer on literary and historical subjects, was elected to the Royal Society of London, and won acceptance at the fashionable dinner tables of French intellectuals.[2] John Adams, after inviting him to dinner in Paris, decided that "Monsieur Raynal is the most eloquent man I ever heard speak in French; his voice is sharp and clear, but pleasant; he talks a great deal, and is very entertaining." Edward Gibbon, the British historian, reported that Raynal's conversation was "intolerably loud, peremptory, and insolent; and you would imagine that he alone was the Monarch and legislator of the World." Horace Walpole, the British gossip, said of Raynal, "There never was such an impertinent and tiresome old gossip." Samuel Johnson is said to have refused to shake hands with him. "Sir," he exclaimed to a friend, "I will not shake hands with an infidel!"[3]

The Abbé Raynal did not have the mentality of Diderot, Voltaire, or a number of other French philosophers of that period, but he had a best-seller. This was *Histoire Philoso-*

2. *Nouvelle Biographie Generale* (Paris, 1866), XLI, 758-66.

3. Diary entry, Feb. 2, 1779, Charles Francis Adams, ed., *The Works of John Adams* (Boston, 1851), III, 186; Gibbon to Lord Sheffield, Sept. 30, 1783, Rowland E. Prothero, ed., *Private Letters of Edward Gibbon (1753-1794)* (London, 1896), II, 75; Walpole's *Correspondence,* VI, 147, 445, cited in John Morley, *Diderot and the Encyclopaedists* (London, 1878), II, 225. Prothero gives Hannah More as the source of the anecdote about Johnson.

phique et Politique, Des Établissements & du Commerce des Européens dans les Deux Indes ("A Philosophical and Political History of the Settlements and Trade of the Europeans in the East and West Indies"). First published in 1770, in six volumes, this work ran through more than twenty authorized editions in French, most of them bearing the names of cities in Holland and Switzerland. It also appeared in more than fifty pirated editions, including many translations into other languages. Teeming with colorful anecdotes and with tirades against churches and governments, the *Histoire* made Raynal perhaps the most widely read author in France, especially after the enlarged 1780 edition was publicly burnt by government order in 1781.[4] This edition forced Raynal to flee France and become an exile.

The book is a rambling account of European penetration into nearly all parts of the globe, including North America. It falls short of being good history, but there is no question about its powerful influence on the French Revolution.[5] John Morley, biographer of Voltaire, Rousseau, and Diderot, concluded that Raynal's *Histoire* "was perhaps, on the whole, the most vigorous and sustained of all the literary expressions that were given to the great social ideas of the century." Mentioning the sentimental passages that sprinkled Raynal's pages, Morley said that none was more popular

4. Edmond Scherer, *Études sur la Littérature au XVIIIe Siècle* (Paris, 1891), 279, 269; August Fournier, *Napoleon the First,* ed., Edward Gaylord Bourne (New York, 1903), 13; Silas Deane to Charles Thomson, Paris, June 1, 1781, Charles Isham, ed., *The Deane Papers* (New York, 1887-1891), IV, 398.

5. Anatole Feugère, *Un Précurseur de la Révolution: L'Abbé Raynal* (Angoulême, 1922), iv, 219; Morley, *Diderot,* II, 222; Scherer, *Études sur la Littérature,* 277, 279.

than the episode of Polly Baker.[6] Polly's speech rode with
the *Histoire* wherever people read books, from the palaces
of emperors to the Haitian slave cabin of Toussaint
L'Ouverture.[7]

Raynal used Polly's courtroom ordeal as an illustration
of the severity of the laws in New England, and he represented the speech as veritable historical fact.[8] He did not
place the trial in Connecticut, as had the British press and
Peter Annet, but only in New England. He failed to give
the date of the trial but stated that it was not very long ago.
After quoting the speech, he reported that the court dis-
pensed with Polly Baker's punishment and, as the very peak
of her triumph, one of the judges married her—"so far is
the voice of reason above powers of studied eloquence."[9]
Nothing was said about the fifteen subsequent children.

The authority for the story was not given, but most of
the text closely followed that of the British magazines of
1747, and it could have been loosely translated from one of
those or from Annet. On the other hand, some new out-
bursts of sentiment were put in Polly's mouth, and nowhere
in sight was her old assertion that a statue ought to be
erected to her memory.

Polly in Raynal's hands was a more overwrought woman
than she had been in her English incarnation. She demanded to know the identity of the barbarous legislator

6. Morley, *Diderot,* II, 234, 239, 242-43. Cf. Yrjö Hirn, "Polly Baker," in
Nya Argus (1913), 19, as quoted by Johansson, *Diderot,* 185n.

7. Morley, *Diderot,* II, 228, 246; Ralph Korngold, *Citizen Toussaint* (Boston,
1944), 61.

8. Polly's speech is in Book 17 of Raynal's *Histoire Philosophique et Politique.*
The pagination varies from one edition to another, but here are the page
references in three of the major editions consulted: Amsterdam (1770), VI,
257-62; La Haye (1774), VI, 330-36; Genève (1780), IV, 241-44.

9. Raynal, *Histoire* (Amsterdam, 1770), VI, 262.

who, pronouncing between the two sexes, favored the stronger and was more severe on that luckless sex which pays for a single pleasure with a thousand dangers and a thousand infirmities. At one point she tactlessly told her judges, "No, gentlemen, heaven is not merciless and unjust, as you are." A little later, presumably with a great rolling of eyeballs, she turned from the magistrates and addressed a long passage to *"Dieu juste & bon"*—"O just and good God, God repairer of evils and injustices, it is to thee I appeal the sentence of my judges. Do not avenge me; do not punish them; but deign to enlighten them and soften them." The concluding sentences were altered in like vein, Polly's parting shot being something like, "I still ask for the punishment that awaits me rather than to hide the fruits of the fertility which heaven gave to man and woman as his first benediction."[10]

During the decade between Raynal's first edition in 1770 and his even more explosive version of 1780, Polly's voice was heard again in England. For example, her speech was printed in an anonymous work appearing in London in 1776 entitled *The History of North America*. This was a translation of the North American portions of Raynal's work, though the title page did not acknowledge that fact.[11] Thus Polly's words were not the original English text at all, but a translation of a translation. In addition, English translations of Raynal's whole *Histoire* were published in Britain. In one, the Polly Baker affair was merely summarized; the speech was omitted on the ground that "this speech is in the

10. *Ibid.,* 260, 262.
11. [Anonymous], *The History of North America. Containing an exact account of their first settlements . . . with the present state of the different colonies* (London, 1776), 82-87.

hands of every English reader, [and] the translator has judged it unnecessary to swell his translation with it."[12]

An odd thing happened in 1777. Some enterprising men in London were publishing two newspapers in the French language, one for distribution in Britain and the other on the Continent. On June 17, both papers printed Polly's oration. They did not mention Raynal. The French text they used was a very close translation of the speech that had appeared in the British press thirty years before. It was not Raynal's translation. A comparison reveals some surprising facts. The speech itself—Miss Baker's own utterance—is identical in both editions, not only textually but also typographically. It undoubtedly was printed in both papers from the same type. But curiously, the two papers did not agree on the name of the heroine. Even more curiously, they gave totally different explanations of how the speech came to their attention.

Ordinarily both publications went under the same title, *Courier de l'Europe* ("European Messenger"), but during a twelve-month period beginning shortly before the printing of Polly's speech, the edition circulated in Britain called itself *Courier Politique et Littéraire* ("Political and Literary Messenger"). In announcing the change to that title on May 23, 1777, the editor (unnamed) assured the British public that he would "be studiously cautious never to start the crimson blush on the maiden cheek of modesty and innocence." His printing of the speech of Polly Baker on June 17 suggests that he either cared little for his pledge or believed that it took more than five bastards to start the crimson

12. Raynal, *A Philosophical and Political History of the Settlements and Trade of the Europeans in the East and West Indies,* trans. J. O. Justamond, 3rd edn. (London, 1777), V, 188.

blush. The editor prefaced the oration with an explanatory paragraph, placed between quotation marks as though copied from another source. In it the reader was told that a provincial paper (unidentified) had reported that an unfortunate girl (presumably English) had given birth to some illegitimate children and been sentenced to a whipping. The reader was then told that the provincial paper had revived the speech of Polly Baker of Connecticut because it was a case of the same sort. The paragraph ended with a bit of propaganda—a claim that barbarous laws still existed in England and a wish that the speech could have the same effect on the legislative body that it had in the mouth of "la Philosophe *Polly*."[13]

Meanwhile the other edition, circulating in Paris and elsewhere on the Continent under the original title, *Courier de l'Europe,* explained to *its* readers that the speech had arrived in a recent letter from America and had been sent to the newspaper by an exceedingly well-known man. The readers were not given the name of this personage, but they were informed that his rank in the world entitled him to "notre profonde vénération."[14] Many a French reader must have immediately assumed this to mean Benjamin Franklin, who had arrived in France six months before to seek help in the war against Britain and whose renown was fabulous. Franklin may have engineered the publication of Polly's speech in *Courier de l'Europe,* perhaps working through the newspaper's Paris office. If he did, he may have known

<hr/>

13. *Courier Politique et Littéraire, Annonces et Avis Divers: Or, French Evening Post,* I, No. 8, 17 juin 1777, 60-61. The "crimson blush" passage in English is in *ibid.,* I, No. 1, 23 mai 1777, 1.

14. *Courier de l'Europe,* II, No. V, 17 juin 1777, 40. See also Alfred Owen Aldridge, *Franklin and His French Contemporaries* (New York, 1957), 102, 245.

quite well that the piece would also be distributed in Britain in *Courier Politique et Littéraire.* If we acknowledge Franklin's hand in the affair, what are we to think of the story given in the paper that an English girl had been condemned to be whipped in accordance with a barbarous English law? Must we not suspect that Franklin's real motive, if it was he who planted the speech, was to take a sly poke at the English? Indeed, Franklin may even have composed or suggested the prefatory paragraph that appeared in *Courier Politique et Littéraire.*

There is a further puzzle in this episode: *Courier de l'Europe,* the Continental edition, gave the heroine's name not as Polly Baker but as Marie Baker! "Marie" is the French equivalent of "Mary." And "Polly" is a nickname for "Mary." Although there is a close kinship between the names "Polly" and "Marie," this does not tell us why the editors used both names.

The Abbé Raynal never called his heroine "Marie," though at one point in his 1780 edition the name appears as "Polli" instead of "Polly." However, there were other changes—far more important than the spelling of Polly's name—in the two major revisions of the *Histoire* in 1774 and 1780, and these changes have assumed a peculiar interest for some scholars in the twentieth century.

In 1774, fourteen lines were dropped out. The deleted passage contained Polly's denunciation of bachelors, which had been a part of the text from the time it first appeared in England.[15] And in 1780, the explanatory material at the end of Polly's discourse was enlarged by a significant inser-

15. *Histoire* (La Haye, 1774), VI, 336.

tion. The new passage said that this speech would be heard often *"dans nos contrées & par-tout où l'on a attaché des idées morales à des actions physiques qui n'en comportent point, si les femmes y avoient l'intrépidité de Polli Baker."*[16] The passage is quoted in French because it contains some interesting language which we will meet again presently. In English, what it says is that the speech would be heard often "in our countries and wherever people have applied moral ideas to physical actions which do not really accord with them, if the women there had the intrepidity of Polli Baker."

The reason these 1774 and 1780 changes are significant is that they seem to lead to the doorstep of a far greater thinker and more gifted talker than Raynal—Denis Diderot. A modern Swedish scholar, Johan Viktor Johansson, has concluded that although Diderot was responsible for the revisions, he had nothing to do with the story as it appeared in Raynal's first edition in 1770.[17]

Others besides Johansson have called attention to the fact that Diderot took some part in the *Histoire*. For example, Raynal's biographer, Anatole Feugère, held it as certain that Diderot was a collaborator in preparing the 1780 edition, probably under a financial contract.[18] But the main circumstance that led Johansson to his opinions about Diderot and Polly was the discovery of an old manuscript that had been lying in a library in Soviet Russia. It was a manuscript of one of Diderot's writings, *Supplément au Voyage de Bougainville*. The Leningrad manuscript differed from all

16. *Histoire* (Genève, 1780), IV, 244.
17. Johansson, *Diderot*, 187-90. Also see Gilbert Chinard's introduction to Diderot's *Supplément au Voyage de Bougainville* (Paris et Baltimore, 1935), 7-8.
18. Feugère, *Raynal*, 187-88.

the previously known texts, and the biggest difference was that it contained Polly Baker's speech.[19]

Denis Diderot (1713-1784) was a man whose vigor of intellect and personality had an unusual effect not only on his contemporaries but also on latter-day scholars. We are told that he would sometimes add an exclamation point to an oral argument by dashing his nightcap passionately against the wall. When he visited Russia, the Empress Catherine the Great wrote to someone in France: "Your Diderot is a very extraordinary man; I always emerge from our discussions with my thighs bruised black and blue; I have been compelled to put a table between us in order to protect myself and my limbs from his gesticulations." But his reputation rests on more than effervescence. He was in charge of one of the greatest works of his century, the thirty-five-volumed *Encyclopédie*. As a thinker, he can be interpreted as having foreshadowed the theory of evolution and other later theories. As a reformer, he was a powerful enemy to artificial or repressive institutions. "No, my dearest," he wrote to a lady friend, "we are not wicked by nature, it is bad education, bad example, bad laws which corrupt us." In acquiring these opinions, he was influenced by English deism. He was also affected by English literature of sentimental analysis. George Lillo's prose tragedy *The London Merchant* impressed him, and Samuel Richardson's novels filled him with enthusiasm.[20]

19. For the French text containing Polly's speech, see Chinard, ed., *Diderot's Supplément;* J. Lough, ed., *Diderot: Selected Philosophical Writings* (Cambridge, England, 1953); or Denis Diderot, *Supplément au Voyage de Bougainville,* ed. Herbert Dieckmann (Genève, Librairie Droz; Lille, Librairie Giard, 1955).

20. Morley, *Diderot,* I, 41, 9, II, 44-45, 51; Edouard Herriott, "Denis

Diderot wrote his *Supplément au Voyage de Bougainville* in 1772. A few years earlier, Louis Antoine de Bougainville had led the first French expedition that circled the globe; he had published a book about it in 1771.[21] At one point Bougainville described his ten-day stopover in Tahiti. Diderot's *Supplément* is a further account of Bougainville's visit to Tahiti, deftly told, humorous, and of course imaginary. The work is in the form of a dialogue between two men, one of whom tells the other about Bougainville's book and relates some incidents which he says Bougainville "suppressed." The subtitle is *Dialogue entre A et B, sur l'inconvénient d'attacher des idées morales à certaines actions physiques qui n'en comportent pas* ("Dialogue between A and B on the disadvantage of applying moral ideas to certain physical actions which do not really accord with them"). This is almost the same language that was inserted into the Polly Baker story in the 1780 edition of Raynal's *Histoire Philosophique et Politique,* and the similarity is one reason for the theory that Diderot wrote the insertion.[22]

As "B" tells it to "A," a crowd of natives are weeping over the impending departure of Bougainville's two ships when an elderly Tahitian steps forth, hushes the mourners, and makes a vehement and eloquent speech. He denounces the Europeans for bringing a sense of shame to the islanders, saying, "Plunge if thou wilt into the dark forest with the perverse partner of thy pleasures, but allow the good and

Diderot," in Romain Rolland, André Maurois, and Edouard Herriott, *French Thought in the Eighteenth Century* (New York, 1953), 266-67; Bonamy Dobrée's introduction in George Lillo, *The London Merchant or The History of George Barnwell* (London, 1948), xii.

21. L. A. Bougainville, *Voyage autour du monde par la frégate du roi "La Boudeuse" et la flûte "L'Etoile" en 1766, 1767, 1768 et 1769.*

22. Johansson, *Diderot,* 189-90.

simple Tahitians to reproduce without shame, in the face of heaven and the open day." "B" then proceeds to tell the experiences of the ship's chaplain who is entertained in the home of a Tahitian named Orou.[23]

Orou, with dignity and courtesy, offers his wife and three daughters to the chaplain, adding that he would be obliged if the chaplain would first choose the youngest daughter, because she has not yet had a child. The chaplain, repeating over and over, "But my religion, but my calling," yields to temptation on four successive nights. He and Orou explain to each other the customs of their respective countries. Orou is bewildered by such terms as "fornication," "adultery," and "incest." European precepts of marriage, he says, are opposed to nature. "Cling to the nature of things and actions," he advises the chaplain. "Thou art mad if thou thinkest there can be anything, high or low, in the universe which can be subtracted from the law of nature." (The real Tahitians were extremely superstitious and priest-ridden, as Bougainville had reported and Diderot very well knew.)[24]

Diderot died in 1784. The *Supplément* first appeared in 1796. It was published again in 1798 and then in various collections during the next century. Those printings contained no mention of Polly Baker.[25]

Suddenly on September 15, 1912, in the columns of the newspaper *Frankfurter Zeitung,* our old friend Polly stood

23. Direct quotations in this and the next paragraph are taken from Francis Birrell, trans., *Dialogues by Denis Diderot* (London, 1927), 122, 126-27, 132, 157-58.

24. Lough, ed., *Diderot,* 176n; Diderot, *Conversation with the Abbé Barthélemy,* as translated by Jean Stewart and Jonathan Kemp in Kemp, ed., *Diderot, Interpreter of Nature: Selected Writings* (London, 1937), 200.

25. Johansson, *Diderot,* 18, 135n.

up and spoke her piece in German. An explanatory note indicated that the speech had been translated not from the *Gentleman's Magazine,* the *London Magazine,* the Abbé Raynal, nor from any of the other known printings, but from Denis Diderot. Nobody, apparently, had ever connected Diderot with Polly during the 128 years that had passed since his death. But the German article said flatly that its version of the speech had been translated from an ancient manuscript of Diderot's *Supplément au Voyage de Bougainville.* And where was this manuscript? It was in Saint Petersburg, Russia.

When this amazing story got around, it caused excitement among European students of literature. Was the most popular episode in Raynal's *Histoire* a literary product of Diderot? Scholars began to take a new interest in Diderot, Raynal, and the words of Polly Baker. Then came World War I and the Russian Revolution. Saint Petersburg became Petrograd, Petrograd became Leningrad, and Johan Viktor Johansson of Sweden became more and more curious about the *Frankfurter Zeitung* article of 1912. During the 1920's he applied himself to the problem. This led him, of course, to Leningrad, and he found the *Supplément* manuscript mentioned in the German newspaper. Though not in Diderot's own handwriting, it was probably made by a copyist near the end of Diderot's life. And sure enough, in the midst of the story about Orou and the French chaplain, "B" interrupts himself to tell "A" about Polly Baker's trial in Connecticut.[26]

The reason for the presence of Diderot's Polly Baker manuscript in Russia is a curious one. In 1765, when the

26. *Ibid.,* 60, 183-84; Dieckmann, ed., *Diderot's Supplément,* xvi-xvii, xxv-xxvi.

time approached for Diderot's daughter to marry, he had no dowry for her. Therefore he determined to sell his library. Catherine the Great heard about his intention. She bought the library, appointed Diderot as the salaried custodian, and paid his salary for fifty years in advance.[27] After his death the library, being Catherine's property, was shipped to her in Saint Petersburg, along with thirty-two volumes of manuscripts. About a century later, in the 1880's, a scholar named Maurice Tourneux visited Saint Petersburg and catalogued the contents of those volumes. But Volume XVII had been mislaid, and it did not turn up until Tourneux had left Russia. Volume XVII contained Diderot's version of Polly's speech, which accordingly remained hidden until the twentieth century.[28]

In 1927 Johansson published a book, *Études sur Denis Diderot* ("Studies on Denis Diderot"), based upon his examination of Volume XVII. Much of the book was devoted to the Polly Baker episode and included information which Johansson learned from sources other than the Leningrad manuscript. According to Herbert Dieckmann of Harvard University, this book marked the beginning of a rebirth of critical writing on Diderot's texts. Thus we see that Miss Baker unwittingly made a contribution to modern scholarship on Diderot.[29]

Dieckmann himself dug into another big cache of Diderot manuscripts and reported the results in 1951. These papers had remained in France after Diderot's death and had been handed down to his descendants. Dieckmann found three more handwritten copies of the *Supplément,*

27. Morley, *Diderot,* I, 289.
28. Johansson, *Diderot,* 26, 59-60.
29. Dieckmann, ed., *Diderot's Supplément,* xxv.

one with Polly Baker and two without. The evidence seemed to show that Diderot first wrote the *Supplément* without Polly in 1772 and inserted her speech in the final version of the piece around 1780.[30]

Only a glance at the Polly Baker stories in Diderot's *Supplément* and Raynal's *Histoire* shows that neither version was copied from the other. Both obviously derived from the English text, but are not the same translation. Diderot accorded with Raynal in suppressing Polly's appeal for a statue. Diderot, however, differed from both Raynal and the British periodicals over the identity of Polly's husband. In his version, it was not one of her judges who married her; it was her original seducer, who heard what happened at the trial and felt so remorseful that "two days later he married Miss Baker, and made an honest woman of her whom five years before he had made a public woman."[31] Thus Diderot raised the banners of justice and romance— but at the expense of humor. The statement that the seduction had taken place five years before, which does not appear in the British texts, is perhaps based on a simple estimate of one baby a year. Diderot, like Raynal, says nothing about the arrival of fifteen more children after the marriage.

Diderot shortened Polly's denunciation of bachelors and caused her to emphasize their crime of seduction rather than their unmarried status. To Johansson, this abridgement indicated that Diderot was the person who deleted the portion on bachelors from the 1774 edition of Raynal's *Histoire*.[32] For our purposes, the question of whether it

30. *Ibid.*, xxii-xxiii, xxvii; Dieckmann, *Inventaire du Fonds Vandeul et Inédits de Diderot* (Genève, 1951), 26-27, 144-45, 146.

31. Chinard, ed., *Diderot's Supplément*, 159.

32. Johansson, *Diderot*, 185-89.

was Diderot who made the alterations in the *Histoire* of
1774 and 1780 is a matter of no great importance. After
all, neither Raynal nor Diderot originated Polly's speech.
The significant fact is that these two radicals considered
Polly useful. With a little French tailoring they worked
her speech into the revolutionary message they were preach-
ing to their age.

In 1782, just seven years before the people of Paris de-
molished the Bastille, the American heroine was embraced
by yet a third French radical, a politician who was to take
a prominent part in the Revolution itself. This was J. P.
Brissot de Warville, an intense and brilliant young man,
more than forty years younger than Raynal and Diderot.

Brissot was born at Chartres in 1754, the son of a restau-
rant keeper. He became a writer of books, entered politics,
founded an influential Paris newspaper, and hurled himself
into the cause of liberty, equality, and the sovereignty of
the people. A biographer has written of him: "In the variety
of his interests and in his unceasing efforts for reform of all
kinds, he suggests Benjamin Franklin, but unlike Franklin,
he had not a vestige of a sense of humor, and took all the
world, including himself, with profound seriousness."[33] In
1788, Brissot traveled in the United States and interviewed,
among others, the aged Franklin. Soon after his return
to France the storm broke, and during the first three years
of the Revolution he was one of the most active participants.
But in 1792 the party he led, the Girondists, fell out of favor.
Brissot and his associates, singing the Marseillaise, rode in
carts to the guillotine. He was thirty-eight years old.

33. Eloise Ellery, *Brissot de Warville* (Boston and New York, 1915), 57.

Brissot was only twenty-eight when he published the speech of Polly Baker. He did this in Volume VIII of a massive work entitled *Bibliothèque Philosophique du Législateur, du Politique, du Jurisconsulte* ("Philosophical Library of the Legislator, the Politician, the Jurist"). A subtitle informed the reader that these volumes contained a selection of the best speeches, dissertations, and essays on criminal legislation, drawn from many countries.[34]

Brissot introduced Polly's speech as an answer to those moralists and politicians who had declaimed against women for daring to become mothers without recourse to marriage. He said the address seemed to him persuasive. He noted that though it had been printed several times it belonged in this collection and might be useful because it dealt with abuses that still existed in most countries. Then Brissot gave the speech itself, after which he added still more comments. Every reasonable man, he was sure, would be persuaded that between a girl who faithfully keeps her chastity and one who renounces hers, the latter is not the less virtuous. He said it was the law of nature for women to work to acquire the title of mother. Why does society contradict this law? Why doesn't it come to the aid of women forced by misfortune into irregular behavior or even into debauchery?

As for the text of Polly's speech, Brissot used a translation that followed neither Raynal's nor Diderot's nor the one printed in *Courier de l'Europe* and *Courier Politique et Littéraire* in 1777. Brissot's translation adhered rather closely in substance to the speech as printed in the British press before he was born. He even retained Polly's bid for a

34. *Bibliothèque Philosophique du Législateur* . . . (Berlin, 1782), VIII, 363-68. Brissot's publishing of the work is discussed by Ellery, *Brissot*, 468 and *passim*.

statue—in fact, not merely one statue, but *statues*. One suspects Raynal and Diderot of quietly burying the statue for the same reason that Edward Cave may have removed Polly's fifteen children from the *Gentleman's Magazine* in 1747, namely that it sounded as if someone was pulling the reader's leg. They may have removed the humorous ending for the simple reason that they did not wish to make Polly a humorous character. Perhaps Brissot was insensitive to leg-pulling.

Diderot died before the French Revolution began. Brissot fell victim to the Terror. The ancient little Abbé Raynal lived on and on, horrified by the bloody turn of the events which he and his best-seller had helped set in motion. He finally died in poverty in 1796. But we have run ahead of our story and must go back to relate how Raynal learned of Polly Baker's true origin.

CHAPTER *Seven*

The *Author Revealed*

ENIS Diderot did not have to answer to the American colonists for putting New England in a bad light, for they never knew he did it. Brissot de Warville probably had very few American readers. But the Abbé Raynal was in a different category. What he wrote about America was widely read, and much of it was violently criticized. George Washington himself called Raynal's writings on America "quite erroneous."[1]

It may seem strange that Raynal, the passionate crusader for liberty, had such a talent for antagonizing the Americans. One reason was that Raynal tended to associate the cause of liberty and justice less with the white settlers than with the Indians. The principal exception was Pennsylvania, which he vaguely linked with William Penn and Benjamin Franklin. In Pennsylvania were to be found "the dawnings of reason, happiness, and humanity, rising from among the ruins of a hemisphere, which still reeks with the blood of all its people, civilized as well as savage."[2]

1. Washington to Richard Henderson, June 19, 1788, John C. Fitzpatrick, ed., *The Writings of George Washington* (Washington, D.C., 1939), XXIX, 522.
2. Raynal, *Philosophical and Political History*, trans. J. O. Justamond (London, 1788), VII, 289.

If Raynal had met Franklin before publishing the early versions of the *Histoire Philosophique et Politique* in 1770 and 1774, he might never have included a sentence which caused him much embarrassment: "It must be a matter of astonishment to find that America has not yet produced a good poet, an able mathematician, or a man of genius in any single art or science."[3]   In the edition of 1780, by which time he had made Franklin's acquaintance in Paris, Raynal eliminated the offending sentence.   He also retracted earlier assertions that the English freemen who had settled in North America had "visibly degenerated," calling this a "fatal prejudice" which, though "universally" held, was incorrect.[4]

Nevertheless it was difficult for Raynal to live down his prior statements.   Thomas Jefferson, in *Notes on Virginia,* written in 1781 and 1782, made a devastating reply to the Abbé's 1774 edition.   He reminded his readers that America was still young, having only three million people to France's twenty million; yet he pointed to Washington in war, Franklin in physics, and Rittenhouse in astronomy.   As late as 1798, according to an English visitor to Mount Vernon, George Washington recalled Raynal as having demanded whether America had yet produced one great poet, statesman, or philosopher.   Washington remarked that America had furnished Franklin, Rittenhouse, and Rush in science, Jefferson and Adams as politicians, and Jonathan Edwards

3. The translation is from *A Philosophical and Political History of the British Settlements and Trade in North America,* from the French of Abbé Raynal, translator not named (Edinburgh, 1776), II, 163.

4. Raynal, *Philosophical and Political History,* trans. J. O. Justamond (London, 1783), VII, 406.   This translation reflected the changes made by Raynal in his 1780 edition.

in polemics. Thus did Jefferson and Washington pay tribute to each other at Raynal's expense.[5]

Raynal drew upon himself yet another heavy bombardment from America, this time from Thomas Paine. Paine, who considered Franklin "a living epitome of all the useful knowledge in the world," had moved to America in 1774 on Franklin's advice and had thrown his writing genius into the cause of independence. His quarrel with Raynal resulted from the fact that Raynal added a history of the American Revolution to his 1780 edition (though the war was still going on). With or without Raynal's connivance this history was separately published in London in 1781, was immediately reprinted in America, and achieved great fame.[6] Paine disliked it intensely on the ground of inaccuracy and unwise judgments—also, incidentally, because Raynal had freely borrowed from Paine's pamphlet *Common Sense* without giving due credit. Therefore, in 1781 and 1782, Paine wrote his *Letter to the Abbé Raynal, on the Affairs of North America.*

Paine, like Franklin, was an ancestor of the modern-day public relations expert. As soon as his reply to Raynal came off the press, he saw to it that copies were sent wherever they would be reprinted and do the most good. He even shipped fifty copies to George Washington "for the use of the army." Robert R. Livingston sent some copies to Franklin in France, and Franklin wrote back that he had "distributed them into good hands." Franklin added: "The

5. Thomas Jefferson, *Notes on the State of Virginia,* ed. William Peden (Chapel Hill, 1955), 64-65; Washington's remark is in John Bernard, *Retrospections of America, 1797-1811* (New York, 1887), 91-92.
6. Raynal, *The Revolution of America* (London, 1781).

errors we see in histories of our times and affairs weaken our faith in ancient history."[7]

By then Raynal had escaped France, one jump ahead of the police, and had begun his exile. But before he left, he received some very surprising news concerning the speech of Polly Baker.

One day at Benjamin Franklin's house in Passy, a suburb of Paris, Dr. Franklin was talking with Silas Deane of Connecticut about the numerous errors in the Abbé Raynal's *Histoire*.

The date of this conversation is uncertain, but it was probably toward the end of 1777 or the beginning of 1778.[8] At this time Franklin had been the American minister in France about a year. He was over seventy, with a tremendous life behind him and much work still to do. The personal fame that had commenced when Edward Cave printed his little book on electricity in 1751 had now assumed heroic proportions. Scientist, inventor, printer, author, tradesman, statesman, patriot, diplomat—Franklin had risen by his own merit to this glittering eminence from a humble birth in Boston as the fifteenth child of a soap-and-candle-maker. To the French he seemed the personification of Reason, Nature, Liberty, and Equality. They adored him. John Adams, who certainly did *not* adore him,

7. Paine's *Letter to the Abbé Raynal* is reprinted in Philip S. Foner, ed., *The Complete Writings of Thomas Paine* (New York, 1945), II, 211-63. Also see Paine to Robert Morris, Sept. 6, and Paine to General Washington, Sept. 7, 1782, *ibid.*, II, 1211-12; Franklin to Robert R. Livingston, Dec. 5, 1782, Albert Henry Smyth, ed., *The Writings of Benjamin Franklin* (New York, 1905-1907), VIII, 635.

8. [Philip Mazzei], *Recherches Historiques et Politiques sur les États-Unis de l'Amérique Septentrionale* (Paris, 1788), III, 23.

and who believed that Franklin's fame was not fully deserved, observed that "his reputation was more universal than that of Leibnitz or Newton, Frederick or Voltaire, and his character more beloved and esteemed than any or all of them."[9]

While Franklin and Deane were talking about Raynal's *Histoire,* the Abbé himself walked into the house. The words that were spoken next we do not know precisely, but we have a second-hand report of them from Thomas Jefferson, who said Franklin told him the story when they were in Paris together (in 1784 or 1785).

After the usual salutations, Jefferson reported, Deane said to Raynal, "The Doctor and myself, Abbé, were just speaking of the errors of fact into which you have been led in your history."

"Oh no, Sir," said the Abbé, "that is impossible. I took the greatest care not to insert a single fact, for which I had not the most unquestionable authority."

"Why," said Deane, "there is the story of Polly Baker, and the eloquent apology you have put into her mouth, when brought before a court of Massachusets to suffer punishment under a law, which you cite, for having had a bastard. I know there never was such a law in Massachusets."

"Be assured," said the Abbé, "you are mistaken, and that that is a true story. I do not immediately recollect indeed the particular information on which I quote it; but I am certain that I had for it unquestionable authority."

Dr. Franklin, who had for some time been shaking with restrained laughter, now entered the conversation: "I will

9. Charles Francis Adams, ed., *The Works of John Adams* (Boston, 1856), I, 660.

tell you, Abbé, the origin of that story. When I was a printer and editor of a newspaper, we were sometimes slack of news, and to amuse our customers, I used to fill up our vacant columns with anecdotes, and fables, and fancies of my own, and this of Polly Baker is a story of my making, on one of those occasions."

The Abbé, without the least embarrassment, exclaimed with a laugh:

"Oh, very well, Doctor, I had rather relate your stories than other men's truths."[10]

Now, if the lesson of this is to be wary of anecdotes, we have to apply the lesson not only to the Polly Baker incident but also to the Jeffersonian account of the conversation in which Franklin confessed authorship of the speech. Even when an anecdote has every appearance of plausibility and comes from such creditable sources as Franklin and Jefferson, it should at least be examined before swallowing. And a close look reveals two statements that are at variance with the facts as known today. It is not certain who was responsible for these inaccuracies. The direct quotations as given above are taken from a writing by Jefferson in 1818, at least thirty-three years after he heard the story from Franklin. Either man could have had slips of memory or colored the anecdote to make it better in the telling.

The first error was the statement attributed to Silas

10. The direct quotations conform verbatim with Jefferson's manuscript in the Library of Congress—an enclosure with a letter to Robert Walsh, Dec. 4, 1818—except that Jefferson started some of his sentences with lower-case letters; also I inserted a comma before "Abbé" at the beginning of the story. The anecdote is printed in Paul Leicester Ford, ed., *The Writings of Thomas Jefferson* (New York, 1899), X, 120-21.

Deane: "I know there never was such a law in Massachusets."

If Deane really made any such contention, he may have said "in New England" rather than "in Massachusetts," because Raynal in his book had not mentioned Massachusetts in connection with Polly Baker. In either event the contention was wrong. Both Massachusetts and Connecticut had laws against fornication, which simply meant sexual intercourse on the part of an unmarried person. Whenever an unwed woman became a mother, this was irrefutable evidence of fornication. The court records of both Massachusetts and Connecticut during the seventeenth and eighteenth centuries contain many cases in which unmarried mothers were fined or whipped. Often these records describe the crime merely as "having a bastard child."[11] The fathers were similarly punished, when they could be identified.

At first, to be sure, the early settlers did not quite know how to punish fornication. When they came to the point of writing laws in Massachusetts, they depended on Moses for guidance on moral offenses. Clearly, the Mosaic penalty for adultery and certain other sex crimes was death. Concerning fornication, however, Moses required only that a man who enticed an unbetrothed maid must marry her, or, if her father would not allow this, the enticer must pay money instead. The Puritans thought the maid should be punished too. They also looked in vain for Biblical authority to apply the lash for fornication. In the absence of a clear mandate, some favored whipping, others only a fine.

11. For example, see the entries of July 15, 1715, and Jan. 1, 1717, in the manuscript Records of the Court of General Sessions of the Peace (Suffolk County Courthouse, Boston).

Written arguments were prepared on both sides of the question.[12]

It was finally decided to leave it to the judges in each case. A law adopted in 1642 said that "if any man Commit Fornication with any single Woman, they shall be punished, either by enjoyning Marriage, or Fine, or Corporal punishment, or all, or any of these, as the Judges of the Court that hath Cognizance of the Cause shall appoint." In Connecticut, nearly identical language was written into that colony's first real code of laws in 1650. This was the general rule that was carried over into the next century in both colonies, though with certain changes on the basis of experience. For example, in Massachusetts by the beginning of the eighteenth century the father of a bastard was legally required to provide maintenance.[13]

The second error in the anecdote handed down by Franklin and Jefferson was the statement attributed to Franklin that he used the speech of Polly Baker to fill a vacant column in his newspaper. Franklin's paper was the *Pennsylvania Gazette,* a weekly. He took it over in 1729, when he was twenty-three years old, and made it into an entertaining sheet. The most readable numbers were those in which he amused his customers with "anecdotes, and fables, and fancies" of his own. Late in life, when memory had dimmed a little, he may have believed that the famous

12. Thomas Hutchinson, *The History of the Colony and Province of Massachusetts-Bay,* ed. Lawrence Shaw Mayo (Cambridge, Mass., 1936), I, 374. On fornication, see Exodus 22: 16, 17; Deuteronomy 22: 28, 29.

13. For the early statutes see *Colonial Laws of Massachusetts, 1672-1686* (Boston, 1890), 54; and J. Hammond Trumbull, ed., *Connecticut Blue Laws* (Hartford, 1876), 87. Massachusetts and Connecticut still have laws against fornication, as do most other states; see Robert Veit Sherwin, *Sex and the Statutory Law* (New York, 1949), Part I, 83.

speech was one of those pieces. Certain writers, in view of the Jefferson anecdote, have stated flatly that the Polly Baker speech was in the *Gazette,* but somehow they always forgot to mention the date on which it appeared. When James Parton published his brilliant life of Franklin in 1864 and became the first of Franklin's biographers to credit him with Polly's speech, he said the article appeared in the *Gazette.* John Bigelow, publishing Franklin's works in 1887, reprinted the speech from Parton and quoted him as saying it was in the *Gazette.* John Bach McMaster, analyzing Franklin as a man of letters, said it was in the *Gazette.* Around the turn of the century, Sydney George Fisher said it was in the *Gazette,* but in a later edition, published in 1926, he changed his mind and said it wasn't. In that same year, however, Phillips Russell said it was, and three years later, so did Bernard Faÿ.[14]

This was rather late to be asserting that the speech appeared in Franklin's paper, because by this time more than one literary detective had hunted for it in the files and had reported that it was strangely absent. For example, when Albert Henry Smyth published *The Writings of Benjamin Franklin* in ten volumes between 1905 and 1907, he included Polly's speech but noted that he had searched the *Pennsylvania Gazette* in vain for it—"It is not there." Smyth said the mystery surrounding its first publication remained "impenetrable." He said he was reprinting it from the

14. Parton, *Life and Times of Benjamin Franklin* (Boston, 1864), I, 219; Bigelow, ed., *The Complete Works of Benjamin Franklin* (New York, 1887), II, 18-22; McMaster, *Benjamin Franklin as a Man of Letters* (Boston, 1887), 70; Fisher, *The True Benjamin Franklin* (Philadelphia, 1898), 139; Russell, *Benjamin Franklin, the First Civilized American* (New York, 1926), 111; Faÿ, *Franklin, the Apostle of Modern Times* (Boston, 1929), 205.

Gentleman's Magazine, which, as we know, published the speech in its issue of April 1747.[15]

An examination of every page of every issue of the *Pennsylvania Gazette* from 1729, when Franklin bought the newspaper, until 1747, when the speech erupted in the British press, reveals no trace of Miss Baker. Nor is she visible in Franklin's *General Magazine,* which he published for six months in 1741.[16] In fact no vestige of the speech can be found in any publication earlier than April 15, 1747, the day it came clattering off the press of the *General Advertiser* at Mr. Woodfall's near the Pump in Little Britain. It would be presumptuous to express certainty that no one will ever dig up an earlier printing. But on the present evidence it is reasonable to assume that the printing in the *General Advertiser* was the first.

How the *General Advertiser* acquired the manuscript is a puzzle that must be tackled in a later chapter. As for the question of why Franklin omitted the piece from his own newspaper in Philadelphia, possible reasons are not hard to find. One reason may have been that the influential members of the community, whose friendship and approval Franklin needed, frowned upon ribaldry. At least he did not publish much racy material in the paper after the 1730's. Another reason may have been religious. Franklin may have withheld Polly from publication because her

15. Smyth, ed., *Writings,* II, 464n. A comparison of Smyth's text with that of the *Gentleman's Magazine* shows that he did not copy it there at all. Between the two versions there are eighteen differences of language, forty of punctuation, two of paragraphing, and still others of spelling, capitalization, and italicization.

16. The Historical Society of Pennsylvania has assembled a complete file of the *Gazette* on microfilm. The *General Magazine* has been published for the Facsimile Text Society by the Columbia University Press (New York, 1938).

robust deism and the brash enlisting of God's authority against the guardians of law and order would have shocked some of his readers and might even have jolted them off his subscription list.[17]

But why should Franklin hesitate to publish the speech when so many periodicals in England carried it, and papers in Boston, New York, and Annapolis besides? Did not these sheets have pious readers, too? Of course they did, and some of their readers no doubt were offended. But the proprietors could print the speech without bearing direct responsibility for having created it, whereas in Philadelphia, we must assume, there were some people who already knew who the author was and many more who would know (or suspect) if he gave space to the piece. To print it in far-off England with a straight face, as though it had actually happened, or to reprint it in Boston, New York, or Annapolis with credit to British sources, was very different from Franklin's either printing or reprinting it in his home community, where he himself would be blamed for originating it.

Franklin had still another good reason for not unveiling Miss Baker in Philadelphia. Franklin and his wife Deborah were at that time rearing as their own son a boy, William, who has been generally supposed—during Franklin's lifetime and ever since—to have been born out of wedlock. Publication might have stimulated the gossips of the town.

17. Franklin knew from experience that this danger was more than a bugbear. On June 10, 1731, he published in the *Pennsylvania Gazette* his remarkable "Apology for Printers" occasioned by his having printed a certain advertisement which had caused him to be accused of "Malice against Religion and the Clergy"; Leonard W. Labaree and Whitfield J. Bell, Jr., eds., *The Papers of Benjamin Franklin* (New Haven, 1959), I, 194-99.

So the speech is missing from the *Pennsylvania Gazette,* either for the reasons suggested or others known only to Franklin, and the anecdote told by Jefferson contains at least two inaccuracies. But Jefferson is not the only reputable person to assure us that he heard from Franklin's own lips that Franklin created the speech.

In October 1955, Whitfield J. Bell, Jr., associate editor of *The Papers of Benjamin Franklin,* was searching in the British Museum for unpublished items pertaining to Franklin. One day he came upon a very long manuscript in French, bound in two volumes. The author's name was nowhere in evidence, but he was obviously a Frenchman of the eighteenth century. The manuscript was a "commonplace book" or "ana," a collection of memorable sayings, ideas, and observations, arranged alphabetically.

In the Frenchman's collection were about twenty anecdotes on Franklin. And one of these had to do with a young woman whose name was given as "Polly Backer." The text of this passage may be translated as follows:

Monsieur Franklin, speaking of the inexactitude of history, told me that he had judged by an example of the small amount of time required to turn a contrived adventure into an accepted fact, and here is this example. The story of Polly Backer, that American girl who, having begotten several children, and having been sentenced to an ignominious punishment, made her defense before her judges, and whom one of her judges married, is a small political and moral piece of fiction, composed by Monsieur Franklin himself around 1740. It was put in the newspapers of the time. People debated from afar in the public papers the truth of the piece, some claiming that it was only a tale, others asserting that the story was real and stating the circumstances in which they had known Polly and the judge who had married her, etc. After some years during which they grew tired of speaking about that, along comes the Abbé Raynal, who recounts this tale in his book. Since then, it is firmly believed. Thirty years were sufficient to change fiction into history.[18]

It seems likely that these old handwritten volumes are the long-lost "ana manuscripts" of the Abbé André Morellet, a witty and convivial priest who was one of Franklin's closest French friends. Their association began in 1772, during a six-month period when both men were in England. It is conceivable that Franklin told Morellet about Polly Baker at that time. If not, he probably did so during his residence in France between 1776 and 1785.[19]

The anecdote in the British Museum does not say Franklin wrote the speech for his newspaper, but only that the speech was printed in the newspapers of the time, as indeed it was. Another point of interest is the mention of a debate in the public papers between those who claimed that the piece was fiction and those who said they knew both Polly and her husband. This reference must be to the controversy

18. British Museum Additional Manuscripts 6134, folio 57b.

19. Morellet, in his published memoirs, mentions his ana manuscripts and the fact that they contain anecdotes about Franklin. See Morellet, *Mémoires,* 2nd edn. (Paris, 1822), I, 202-5, 300. He also says that in 1790 (after Franklin's death) he sent some of those very anecdotes to the *Moniteur.* In the July 15, 1790, issue of *Gazette Nationale, ou Le Moniteur Universal* there are ten Franklin anecdotes, presumably by Morellet. Polly Baker is not mentioned. Carl Van Doren found these anecdotes in the *Moniteur* and summarized five of them in his *Franklin,* 649-50, attributing them to Morellet. A comparison of the ten *Moniteur* anecdotes with those in the commonplace book in the British Museum indicates that they were by the same writer.

in the *Gentleman's Magazine* between "William Smith," who said Polly was married to Paul Dudley, and "L. Americanus," who denied it. Thus we now have evidence that Franklin read this hilarious exchange of letters, though the evidence is scarcely needed, for it is most unlikely that such a well-informed reader of current periodicals as Franklin would have missed it.

Indeed, someone has even suggested that Franklin himself was responsible for the letter which put the finger on old Judge Dudley. A modern writer, Christopher Rolfe, referred to the William Smith letter as "inspired, it is believed, by Franklin."[20] Rolfe did not elaborate this statement nor support it with any evidence. Nevertheless the possibility is so intriguing that it warrants a brief examination here. It will be recalled that Edward Cave's *Gentleman's Magazine* printed Polly's speech in its issue of April 1747, the William Smith letter in the May issue, and the "L. Americanus" letter in the June issue. So one fact is immediately clear: Franklin, being in America at the time, could not possibly have written the William Smith letter *after* seeing the April issue, since the April issue did not reach America until July. But suppose Franklin knew long in advance that the speech was going to appear in the London periodicals. Armed with this knowledge, could he not have arranged with someone in London to watch for it, and, when it appeared, to augment the joke by writing a letter claiming to have seen the celebrated Polly Baker? Well, yes, he could, for he was ingenious at literary jokes and pseudonymous letter-writing. Furthermore, having begun his career in Boston, he undoubtedly remembered Paul

20. Rolfe, "Ben Franklin's Polly Baker," the *Mentor*, 11 (June 1923), 38-39.

Dudley and perhaps considered him fair game for a joke. Twenty-five years before "William Smith," some uncomplimentary allusions to Dudley had appeared in the *New-England Courant,* published by the Franklin brothers, James and Benjamin.[21] But this is scarcely proof that Benjamin engineered the elaborate transatlantic libel of 1747.

There can be no reasonable doubt, however, that Franklin was the prankster who invented the speech of Polly Baker. If any additional scraps of testimony were needed, we would have them in letters written by John Adams and William Franklin. In 1783, Adams wrote from Paris concerning Benjamin Franklin: "His whole Life has been one continued Insult to good Manners and to Decency. His Son, and Grandson, as he calls him with characteristic Modesty; the Effrontery with which he has forced these his Offspring up in the World, not less than his Speech of Polly Baker, are Outrages to Morality and Decorum, which would never have been forgiven in any other American."[22] In 1807, seventeen years after Benjamin Franklin's death, William Franklin said in a letter from London that his father "wrote and printed a Piece called the Speech of *Polly Baker,* a young Woman supposed to have had several natural Children."[23] These words hold a special interest coming from one who has been generally considered a natural child himself.

21. Shipton, *Sibley's Harvard Graduates,* IV, 45, 48-49.

22. Adams to James Warren, April 13, 1783, *Warren-Adams Letters,* II (Massachusetts Historical Society, *Collections,* 73 [1925]), 209.

23. William Franklin to Jonathan Williams, July 30, 1807; quoted by permission of Indiana University, which owns the manuscript. Jack C. Barnes of the University of Maryland kindly directed my attention to this letter. William may have been mistaken about Franklin's printing the essay, since it cannot be found in Franklin's newspaper or magazine.

Even without the information given us by Jefferson, Morellet, Adams, and William Franklin, we would still have to suspect Benjamin of creating Polly's discourse. It is couched in the sly and satirical style that he cultivated and used in many other literary hoaxes. Franklin was a skillful and inveterate hoaxer from his precocious teens till his death. Let us quickly examine ten of his literary frauds in the manner of Polly Baker.

(1) At sixteen he wrote the "Silence Dogood" papers in imitation of the *Spectator,* posing as a cheerful country widow and even fooling his brother, who published the letters without knowing who wrote them.[24]

(2) At twenty-four he printed in his own Philadelphia paper a delightful account (wholly or partly fictitious) of a witch trial at Mount-Holly, New Jersey.[25]

(3) At twenty-six, writing as "Poor Richard" Saunders, he satirized astrology and sent his almanac off to a successful start by predicting that a star-gazer and rival almanac-maker named Titan Leeds would meet inexorable death at a certain hour and minute.[26]

(4) In his fifties he enjoyed creating a sensation in English drawing rooms—and striking a blow for toleration—by pretending to read a chapter from Genesis telling how the Lord rebuked Abraham for thrashing a stranger who refused to worship. The chapter was fictitious. Franklin never

24. *New-England Courant,* April 2 to Oct. 8, 1722. The Dogood essays are reprinted in Labaree and Bell, eds., *Papers of Franklin,* I, 8-45.

25. *Pennsylvania Gazette,* Oct. 22, 1730. Reprinted in Labaree and Bell, eds., *Papers of Franklin,* I, 182-83.

26. Preface to *Poor Richard, 1733,* published in December 1732. Reprinted in Labaree and Bell, eds., *Papers of Franklin,* I, 311. Franklin carried on this joke for years. Jonathan Swift had perpetrated just such a hoax in England twenty-five years before, in his "Predictions for the Year 1708."

claimed to have originated the idea, only the style.[27]

(5) In 1761, concerned lest England make peace with France before the French power had been definitely removed as an obstacle to the colonies' expansion, he cleverly combatted peace propaganda by publishing in London what purported to be a pertinent extract from an old Spanish book.[28]

(6) At fifty-nine he ridiculed the foolish items about America that appeared in the London press by publishing a satirical letter, signed "A TRAVELLER," in which he pretended to rush to the defense of the news writers. This letter contains Franklin's well-known assertion that "the grand Leap of the Whale in that Chace up the Fall of Niagara is esteemed by all who have seen it, as one of the finest Spectacles in Nature!"[29]

(7) At sixty-two he deceived many London readers—and shot satirical arrows at various targets—with a long, entertaining extract from a non-existent book supposed to have been written by one William Henry after six years of captivity among the American Indians.[30]

27. An amusing account of this "Parable Against Persecution," as it came to be called, and a good text of it are given by William Strahan in the *London Chronicle*, April 17, 1764. See also a pamphlet by Luther S. Livingston, *Benjamin Franklin's Parable Against Persecution with an Account of the Early Editions* (Cambridge, Mass., 1916). Another text is found in Smyth, ed., *Writings*, VI, 254-56; for another example of how Franklin used the "Parable," see *ibid.*, I, 179-80.

28. The fictitious extract was entitled "Of the Meanes of disposing the Enemie to Peace." See Crane, *Franklin's Letters to the Press*, 18-19. Full text is in *London Chronicle*, Aug. 13, 1761. A slightly different text, taken from a manuscript draft of the piece, is in Smyth, ed., *Writings*, IV, 89-95.

29. *Public Advertiser*, May 22, 1765. Reprinted in full with an interesting discussion by Crane, *Franklin's Letters to the Press*, 30-35. A text taken from a draft of the letter is in Smyth, ed., *Writings*, IV, 367-70.

30. Alfred Owen Aldridge, "Franklin's Deistical Indians," American Philosophical Society, *Proceedings*, 94 (1950), 398-410. Aldridge found the account in the *London Chronicle* of June 25 and June 28, 1768.

(8) At sixty-seven he had Englishmen wryly smiling at his "Edict by the King of Prussia," in which Frederick the Great purportedly imposed a long list of severe restrictions on British trade.[31]

(9) At seventy-six, while in France, he propagandized against England by printing on his private press a fraudulent "Supplement to the Boston Independent Chronicle," reporting the taking of 1,062 American scalps by Indians acting on behalf of King George III.[32]

(10) At eighty-four, just three weeks before his death, he propagandized against slavery by publishing in a Philadelphia newspaper a speech purporting to have been delivered by an Algerian a hundred years before, warmly defending the practice of capturing Christians at sea and selling them into bondage.[33]

Franklin left his handprint not only on the style and method of Polly Baker's speech but also on the substance of it. The essay combines a New England locale with a theme that ran strongly through the English literature and journalism of that day, namely the theme of seduction. Franklin combined in his person a New England background and an intimate familiarity with the English writing of the period. In the next chapter we shall examine some of the contemporary influences that may have affected Franklin when he sat down to be Polly's ghost writer.

31. *Public Advertiser,* Sept. 22, 1773, and *London Chronicle,* Sept. 23, 1773. A text taken from a reprinting in the *Gentleman's Magazine,* 43 (1773), 513-14, is in Smyth, ed., *Writings,* VI, 118-124; an amusing letter that Franklin wrote concerning this hoax is in *ibid.,* 144-47.

32. For a concise discussion see Van Doren, *Franklin,* 671-73. A copy of the *Supplement* is in the Library of Congress. A more convenient (though not strictly verbatim) text is in Smyth, ed., *Writings,* VIII, 437-47.

33. *Federal Gazette and Philadelphia Evening Post,* March 22, 1790. A substantially accurate version is in Smyth, ed., *Writings,* X, 87-91.

CHAPTER Eight

Polly's Origins

IN Worcester, Massachusetts, one August day in 1733, twelve justices of the Court of General Sessions of the Peace assembled for their quarterly meeting to hear charges against certain residents of Worcester County for such crimes as absenting themselves from church, traveling on Sunday (or Saturday night after sunset), "prophanely swearing," and fornication. One of the defendants was an unmarried woman named Eleonor Kellog, who lived in the town of Brookfield. She confessed that she had become a mother, whereupon the court ordered her to pay a fine of five pounds or be whipped ten stripes. She paid and was discharged. If her judges suspected that they had not seen the last of her, they were entirely correct.

Miss Kellog was prosecuted again in May 1737 for "comitting ye crime of fornication," says the court record, "having had a bastard child born of her body sometime in ye month of July 1736." This time she pleaded not guilty, but the court was unimpressed and decreed that she must pay a fine or be "severely" whipped. The record does not say whether she paid the fine or submitted to the lash.

She was back again in November 1740, and now the authorities threw the book at her. They put her on trial three consecutive times. First, she was charged with having a bastard child about October 1737 (only five months after her last trial). She admitted this, though at first she may have denied it, for the clerk reported a plea of "not guilty" and struck emphatically through the "not." The court, no longer in a mood to give her a choice of punishments, ordered that she be whipped at some public place in Worcester on the naked body between the hours of one and three of the clock on Saturday, November 8. Second, she was charged with having another bastard child in about April or May 1740. The clerk did not report how she pleaded, only that she was ordered to be whipped for this offense at the same time and place as for the other. Third, she was tried for "willingly willfully and unecessaryly absenting herself from ye Publick Worship of God on Lords days against the peace." She confessed and was fined twenty shillings. In all three trials she was required to pay the cost of prosecution.

But even this ordeal did not stop the headlong public career of Eleonor Kellog. Five years later, when the court convened on Tuesday the fifth of November, 1745, she was waiting in the wings to make her entrance. Nine justices were present; four of them had been on the bench at her first trial twelve years before. The justices heard the charge: "the crime of fornication." According to the record, the defendant "came into Court confessed the fact and this being the fifth crime the Court order that shee be seveerly & publickly whip'd at ye whiping post on the Naked back between the Hours of Nine & Twelve of the Clock the sixth

Instant." The court also ordered that she pay fees and be committed until sentence be performed—"& it was accordingly done."[1]

Less than a year and a half later, the speech of Polly Baker appeared in the London newspapers. Polly, like Eleonor, was prosecuted five times for having bastard children. Polly surpassed Eleonor by making a speech and marrying one of her judges; at least the Worcester court records tell nothing about such events. The records, however, do contain the tantalizing information that one of Eleonor's judges—in her first trial—was a man named Dudley.

On that occasion, in 1733, the list of justices on hand included Samuel Dudley, Esq. When Eleonor was tried the second time in 1737, this name was no longer on the list, but in the very next case after hers, Samuel Dudley, Esq. of the town of Sutton in Worcester County was prosecuted on a charge of "Prophane Swearing." He pleaded to the insufficiency of the presentment, whereupon the court quashed the case, and Dudley paid the cost of the trial. The court record says nothing more.

Investigation reveals that Samuel Dudley was a big property owner, possibly a distant relative of Chief Justice Paul Dudley. This Samuel is not to be confused with the Reverend Samuel Dudley, Paul Dudley's uncle who married

1. Eleonor Kellog's troubles are preserved in the handwritten records of the Court of General Sessions of the Peace, Worcester County, now in the office of the County Commissioners in the Worcester County Courthouse. The quotations are from that source. Her 1733 and 1737 trials are in the volume entitled County Commissioners Records 1731-1737, 34, 98. Her 1740 and 1745 trials are in Sessions Vol. 2, Beg. August 1737, Ends Nov. 1757, 65, 159. I was led to these records by a brief reference to the 1740 and 1745 whippings in an article by Henry Bamford Parkes, "Morals and Law Enforcement in Colonial New England," *New England Quarterly*, 5 (1932), 447.

a daughter of Governor Winthrop. Samuel Dudley of Sutton once represented his town in the Massachusetts Assembly, and his name appears often in the town records until 1737, when it strangely drops out of sight. He moved to Douglas, Massachusetts, about 1745. He married four times. We are told that his eleventh child, born in 1721, was named Paul. This Paul, if he lived, was twenty-five years old when "William Smith" asserted that Polly Baker had married Paul Dudley of Roxbury; but perhaps he did not live, for the church records of Sutton show that Samuel Dudley was the father of another Paul, baptized in November 1732, a child that we might assume belonged to Samuel's eldest son, Samuel Dudley, Jr., except that the church records state clearly that Samuel, Jr., was the father of a boy, Stephen, baptized in June 1732.[2]

Whether or not this bewildering genealogy had anything to do with "William Smith's" erroneous assertions is not known. In any case, the central question is this: Could Franklin in Philadelphia have somehow heard about Eleonor Kellog and thereby got the idea for Polly's fictitious speech? No mention of the Kellog case can be found in colonial newspapers, and indeed it was not the sort of news they usually printed.[3] But Franklin could have learned of it by letter or by word of mouth. This much can be said:

2. Biographical information is from Dean Dudley, *History of the Dudley Family* (Wakefield, Mass., 1891?), 558-59; and from William A. Benedict and Hiram A. Tracy, *History of the Town of Sutton, Massachusetts, from 1704 to 1786* (Worcester, 1878), I, 42ff. (text of town records), and II, 635-36. Church records are given in *Vital Records of Sutton, Massachusetts* (Worcester, 1907), 56, 57.

3. In the search for Eleonor Kellog, the following papers were examined: *Boston Evening-Post, Boston Weekly News-Letter, New England Weekly Journal, New-York Evening-Post, Weekly New-York Post-Boy, Pennsylvania Gazette, Pennsylvania Journal or Weekly Advertiser.*

If he knew nothing about the Worcester affair, the publication of Polly's speech so soon after Eleonor's fifth bastard was a pretty big coincidence.

Coincidences do happen, though, and Franklin may have drawn only upon his knowledge of earlier cases. At the time of his childhood in Boston, numerous New England women, often in the servant class, paid the penalty for fornication. Some of them were repeaters, and we may imagine that instances of notorious fruitfulness entered the lore of the region. Franklin was born in 1706. The records of Hartford County, Connecticut, show that in September 1707, Hannah Trace of Middletown "freely Confessed her Self to be guilty of Fornication, and that Shee hath now had four Bastard Children." Her sentence was to pay a fine of five pounds and provide twenty pounds surety for good behavior. She named William Hamlin as the father, and the court ordered him to contribute to the child's support for four years. At Boston in 1709, Hannah Hurd, appearing for her second fornication trial in about four years, accused "Dick," a Negro man, of being the father. The justices, including Paul Dudley, sentenced her to twenty stripes. There were even some real-life Bakers among those punished for fornication in Boston while Franklin lived there. One was Abijah Baker, who was fined in 1713. Another was Grace Baker, who was fined in 1717 but had the satisfaction of hearing John Jones declared to be the father and sentenced to pay her three shillings a week.[4]

4. Records, Court of Common Pleas, County of Hartford, 1706-1717, 23 (Connecticut State Library, Hartford); Records of the Court of General Sessions of the Peace, 1702-1712, 100, 186, and 1712-1719, 9, 141 (Suffolk County Courthouse, Boston).

This is not to say that young Franklin knew of all such cases, but he was far from being a sheltered boy and we can be certain that he became aware of them in general. When he was sixteen his brother's newspaper, the *New-England Courant,* on which he was working as an apprentice printer, published an anonymous letter about a fornication trial in the very issue—April 16, 1722—that contained one of Franklin's earliest known writings, the second of his "Silence Dogood" papers. The letter began with these words: "Being lately at the Quarter-Sessions, when a certain Lawyer came upon his Tryal for cohabiting with a French Tayloress as his Wife without being married according to the Laws of this Province. . . ." It is also interesting to recall the circumstances of Franklin's departure from Boston at age seventeen. Deciding to leave town secretly in order to escape his brother's control, he enlisted the help of a ship captain by pretending (through an intermediary) that he had "got a naughty girl with child" and was running away in order to avoid marrying her.[5]

The New England that Franklin left behind him provided a setting for Polly's speech, but Old England contributed much to what she said. A horde of poor young women struggling to preserve their virtue with only occasional success inhabit the pages of English literature from Steele and Addison to the mid-century novelists. Franklin was familiar with this growing sentimental strain.

To begin with, he read the essays of Steele and Addison. In fact he learned to write by consciously imitating them, as he tells us in his autobiography. As a teen-ager he met

5. Franklin's Autobiography, Smyth, ed., *Writings*, I, 249-50.

with the third volume of the *Spectator,* delightedly "read it over and over," took notes on some of the essays and, without looking at the book, tried to reconstruct them. "Then," says he, "I compared my *Spectator* with the original, discovered some of my faults, and corrected them." He also turned some of the pieces into verse, and after a time, when he had pretty well forgotten the prose, turned them back again.[6] The third volume contained essays by Steele about women who had been deluded by the male sex. It contained another essay in which Addison attacked the fathers of bastards and humorously proposed that they be banished to the American colonies in order to people those dominions; and there was still another essay in which he wrote that if women were permitted to plead in the courts they would carry eloquence to new heights.[7]

Franklin also read Defoe, and mentions *Moll Flanders* in his autobiography. It seems very likely that he was acquainted with the depraved women in Gay's *The Beggar's Opera,* Lillo's *The London Merchant,* and Hogarth's *A Harlot's Progress.*[8]

Besides, as a newspaper proprietor he regularly read— and copied from—the English newspapers and magazines. It was in 1731 that Henry Baker published in his weekly journal, the *Universal Spectator,* an essay containing a "petition" from 30,000 unmarried women who yearned to enter into wedlock. Franklin may have seen the essay there. If not, he probably saw it as reprinted in the *Gentleman's*

6. *Ibid.,* 241-42.
7. *Spectator,* Nos. 182, 190, 203, 247. See pages 8-9, above.
8. Smyth, ed., *Writings,* I, 251. When Hogarth died in 1764 he had just finished drafting a reply to an agreeable letter from Franklin. See Austin Dobson, *Eighteenth Century Vignettes,* 1st ser. (New York, 1923), 282.

Magazine, for he followed that periodical faithfully, borrowed from it frequently, and once told a friend that he considered it "by far the best."[9] He could also have seen the piece in 1736 when the essays from the *Universal Spectator* were published in book form.

Henry Baker's "petitioners" said they were "under great Uneasiness of Mind, for not fulfilling *God*'s first Command, *increase and multiply,* which they believe their indispensible and bounden Duty." Polly Baker said that nothing had been able to deter her from the steady performance of "the Duty of the first and great Command of Nature, and of Nature's God, *Encrease and Multiply.*"[10]

Thus Baker and Franklin gave new twists to one of the oldest ideas ever put on paper. The Bible says that God, even before the advent of man, blessed the water creatures and the winged fowls, saying, "Be fruitful and multiply." When man came into existence—male and female—"God blessed them, and God said unto them, Be fruitful, and multiply, and replenish the earth."[11] When Franklin caused Polly to lay hold of the injunction, it was not the only time that he turned the "increase and multiply" theme into comedy. In France at age seventy-two, he addressed the following light-hearted passage to one of his dear French friends, Madame Brillon: "People commonly speak of *Ten* Commandments. I have been taught that there are *twelve.* The *first* was, *Increase and multiply* and replenish the Earth.

9. Franklin to William Strahan, Nov. 27, 1755, Smyth, ed., *Writings,* III, 303. The spinsters' petition, after appearing in the *Universal Spectator* of Feb. 13, 1731, was in the *Gentleman's Magazine* for February of that year.

10. Baker's quotation is from his *Universal Spectator* of Feb. 13, 1731, as reprinted in book form in *The Universal Spectator,* 3rd edn. (London, 1756), II, 242. Polly's passage is from *General Advertiser,* April 15, 1747.

11. King James version, Genesis 1: 22, 28. See also Genesis 9: 1; 35: 11.

The *twelfth* is, A new Commandment I give unto you, *that ye love one another*. It seems to me that they are a little misplac'd, and that the last should have been the first. However, I never made any Difficulty about that, but was always willing to obey them both whenever I had an Opportunity."[12]

Henry Baker's unmarried petitioners and their American cousin Polly had more in common than their insistence that multiplying was a religious duty. For example, they agreed in deploring the fact that custom gave men the exclusive privilege of professing love and proposing marriage; they bitterly criticized the men for neglecting to use this privilege; and they joined in a shrill demand that bachelors be fined. Their assault on bachelorhood was not unusual in English journalism, which produced a good deal of hullabaloo on the subject, often in light vein yet reflecting a serious concern. Franklin's own concern is illustrated by the following passage which he wrote to his wife from England in 1760: "The Accounts you give me of the Marriages of our friends are very agreeable. I love to hear of every thing that tends to increase the Number of good People. You cannot conceive how shamefully the Mode here is a single Life. One can scarce be in the Company of a Dozen Men of Circumstance and Fortune, but what it is odds that you find on enquiry eleven of them are single."[13]

12. Franklin to Mme. d'Hardancourt Brillon, dated Passy, March 10, 1778, Leonard W. Labaree and Whitfield J. Bell, Jr., eds., *Mr Franklin, a Selection from His Personal Letters* (New Haven, 1956), 43-44. The editors point out that the relationship between Franklin and Madame Brillon was almost certainly platonic.

13. Franklin to Mrs. Deborah Franklin, June 27, 1760, Smyth, ed., *Writings*, IV, 24.

Polly Baker said of the New England bachelors that by their manner of living they "leave unproduced (which is little better than Murder) Hundreds of their Posterity to the Thousandth Generation." This expression is interesting because Franklin used it on other occasions.[14] In fact, one modern critic, Alfred Owen Aldridge, in a chapter entitled "Polly Baker" in his *Franklin and His French Contemporaries,* writes that the only serious theme in Polly's speech is "philoprogenitiveness—the typically eighteenth-century fondness for fecundity and procreation as such." Aldridge then remarks, "Franklin throughout his life, both humorously and seriously, in bagatelles, in works on economic theory, in personal letters, and in practice consistently stressed the value of an augmented population."[15] This is true enough, though Aldridge's words "in practice" carry more humor than force, inasmuch as only two or three children can be convincingly ascribed to the philoprogenitive Franklin, whereas his father had seventeen and his grandfather nine.

Polly was in no way a plagiarism of Henry Baker's essay of 1731, for she was a New England girl quite different in word and deed from Baker's English spinsters. Franklin's piece is more subtle, satirical, and humorous. Still, Franklin may have drawn some ideas from Baker's essay. It is even remotely possible that he named his heroine after Baker.

Beginning with the Abbé Morellet, a number of writers and editors have faced the problem of the date of Polly's composition. Morellet vaguely named 1740 as the approxi-

14. *Ibid.,* II, 371, III, 359.
15. Alfred Owen Aldridge, *Franklin and His French Contemporaries* (New York, 1957), 97.

mate time, and his guess is probably significant in one respect: this was the year Samuel Richardson's novel of attempted seduction, *Pamela,* exploded on the English scene. The tremendous vogue of this harrowing chronicle may have contributed to Franklin's impulse to amuse himself with a variation of the seduction theme. Franklin's familiarity with *Pamela* is proved by the fact that he published an American edition of it in 1744—the first novel ever printed in America.[16]

The estimates of later scholars are widely varied. None of them knew of Morellet's commonplace book nor of Eleonor Kellog. In 1864, James Parton cited no date but linked the speech with another writing which he ascribed to Franklin and which appeared in the *Pennsylvania Gazette* in 1737,[17] and he left the impression that the oration belonged to the 1730's. John Bach McMaster seemed to think it was written in the 1730's, though he obviously did not know. Rupert Hughes placed it in 1734, without saying why. John Bigelow, though merely reprinting the speech from Parton and quoting what Parton had said about it, chose the year 1745. Phillips Russell implied that it was published about 1729 or 1730, but later in the same book he said the piece belonged to the period of 1745. Howard Payson Arnold guessed that it had first appeared in America within three years before April 1747, though he admitted that he had caused "a most complete and exhaustive search" to be made of "every contemporary journal, magazine, or book which would be in the remotest degree likely to contain the advent of 'Polly Baker,' . . . without the faintest

16. Van Doren, *Franklin,* 103.
17. "The Drinker's Dictionary," in the *Pennsylvania Gazette* of Jan. 13, 1737. See Parton, *Franklin,* I, 218-25.

gleam of suggestion, even, as to its origin." Gilbert Chinard said the first printing was in an American magazine about 1745, though he acknowledged that no one had ever found it. Albert Henry Smyth, editing *The Writings of Benjamin Franklin,* confessed that it was impossible to date the speech; so he deposited it, dateless, in an appendix.[18]

Carl Van Doren classed Polly's speech among Franklin's "surreptitious writings" and implied that it was written in 1745 or 1746, along with the famous "Advice to a Young Man on the Choice of a Mistress," which was dated June 25, 1745.[19] His version of Polly's date is probably the most accurate approximation which has been made. Perhaps we can be even more specific. We have seen that Eleonor Kellog's fifth fornication trial took place in November 1745 and that Polly's speech was published in April 1747. In view of the trial (of which Van Doren knew nothing), it seems a good guess, though not at all a certainty, that Franklin wrote the speech in 1746.

Indeed, Van Doren had good cause to associate it with "Advice to a Young Man on the Choice of a Mistress." Several textual similarities show an affinity between the two pieces close enough to suggest at least that they were written during the same period of Franklin's life.

In "Advice to a Young Man" Franklin began by praising marriage as "the most natural State of Man, and therefore the State in which you are most likely to find solid Happiness." He said that a single man "is an incomplete Animal.

18. McMaster, *Franklin,* 70-71, 93; Hughes, "Washington, Franklin, Adams, Hamilton, Jefferson," in John Macy, ed., *American Writers on American Literature* (New York, 1931), 45; Bigelow, *Works of Franklin,* II, 18-22; Russell, *Franklin,* 111, 103, 170; Arnold, *Historic Side-lights,* 151; Chinard, ed., *Diderot's Supplément,* 154n; Smyth, ed., *Writings,* II, 464n.

19. Van Doren, *Franklin,* 150-54.

He resembles the odd Half of a Pair of Scissars.—If you get a prudent healthy Wife, your Industry in your Profession, with her good Oeconomy, will be a Fortune sufficient."[20]

(Said Polly Baker: "I must be stupified to the last Degree, not to prefer the Honourable State of Wedlock, to the Condition I have lived in. I always was, and still am willing to enter into it; and doubt not my behaving well in it, having all the Industry, Frugality, Fertility, and Skill in Oeconomy, appertaining to a good Wife's Character.")[21]

In the "Advice to a Young Man," Franklin went on to say that if the young man would not take the counsel of marriage, and persisted in having amours, he should *"prefer old Women to young ones."* Franklin then gave eight reasons for this. Only two of them need be quoted here— not that they are the most remarkable or entertaining, but they are the most pertinent to the history of Polly Baker.

The third reason: "Because there is no hazard of Children, which irregularly produc'd may be attended with much Inconvenience." (Polly Baker's children, irregularly produced, caused her not only the inconvenience of maintaining them by her own industry, without a husband's support, but also the inconvenience of five arrests, five court trials, two heavy fines, and two public whippings.)

The sixth reason: "Because the Sin is less. The debauching a Virgin may be her Ruin, and make her for Life unhappy." (Polly Baker, when a virgin, trusted a man who

20. Franklin called this piece "The Old Mistresses' Apologue." An edition of it was published under that title at Philadelphia in 1956 by the Philip H. & A. S. W. Rosenbach Foundation, with an editorial note by Whitfield J. Bell, Jr. The quotations here are from that source.

21. *General Advertiser,* April 15, 1747.

got her with child and then forsook her. He was the first cause of all her faults and misfortunes, which continued, perhaps not "for Life" in her case, but at least until one of her judges married her—a happy ending which mere mortals like Eleonor Kellog could hardly hope for.)

Franklin reached the age of forty in January 1746. Carl Van Doren, after summarizing Polly's arguments, wrote the following: "It is hardly accident that Franklin's salty year came when, just before and after forty, he had at last a clear sense of the leisure toward which he had long been working. It is no wonder that his spirits rose or that in cheerful moments he amused himself and his friends with philosophical ribaldries."[22]

More than a century after Franklin's "salty year," two distinguished and high-minded Americans published violently contrasting views about Franklin, and each of them used the speech of Polly Baker to support his opinion. In 1856, Charles Francis Adams, the grandson of John Adams and the man who was later to become Abraham Lincoln's minister to Great Britain, cited the speech as evidence that Franklin lacked "that nice sense which revolts at wrong for its own sake, and that generosity of spirit which shrinks from participating in the advantages of indirection." Adams's righteous eye had happened to fall upon Thomas Jefferson's anecdote in which Franklin informed the Abbé Raynal that he had thought up the story to pad out his newspaper. Adams attacked Franklin not only for writing the speech but also for betraying the "levity of such a reason

22. Van Doren, *Franklin*, 154-55.

as he gave for disseminating its unworthy sophistry in print."[23]

James Parton, bringing out his *Life and Times of Benjamin Franklin* in 1864, answered Adams as follows: "This is highly absurd. John Adams's own grandson speaks in these words; though I hardly think the indomitable old patriot could have been so insensible to a joke as to talk in that priggish way of Polly Baker." (In this statement, however, Parton misjudged the "indomitable old patriot," not being aware that Adams had condemned Polly's speech as an outrage to morality long before his grandson was born.) Parton maintained that the speech "is not only humorous, but well rebukes the cruel immorality which sent a poor miserable drab to the whipping-post, and invited her seducer to dinner." Elsewhere in his book Parton called Franklin "the consummate Christian of his time." He went even further: "Indeed, I know not who, of any time, has exhibited more of the spirit of Christ. . . . He was tolerant of every thing but intolerance, and made some charitable allowance even for that. At poor Polly Baker, he had not a stone to throw. . . . He went about the world doing good."[24]

Both C. F. Adams and Parton, though miles apart in their views, saw Polly's speech as an expression of Franklin's character. In the twentieth century a new discovery was announced, namely that Polly was none other than Franklin in disguise.

23. Charles Francis Adams, *Works of John Adams,* I, 319. C. F. Adams had seen Jefferson's anecdote in H. A. Washington, ed., *The Writings of Thomas Jefferson* (Washington, D.C., 1854), VIII, 501-2. Jefferson had enclosed this and other anecdotes with a letter to Robert Walsh, Dec. 4, 1818.

24. Parton, *Franklin,* I, 219-21, II, 400, 646. For Adams's condemnation of Polly Baker's speech, see above, p. 90.

This brings us again to William Franklin, the son in the Franklin household. William in later life became royal governor of New Jersey and broke with his father when they chose different sides in the Revolution. At the time of the writing of Polly's speech, William was probably fifteen or sixteen years old. Benjamin had married Deborah Read Rogers on September 1, 1730. William seems to have been born sometime before April 12, 1731. He is commonly said to have been Franklin's son by an unknown mother, though there is also a theory that he was Deborah's by an unknown father. The assumption that he was illegitimate seems a permanent fixture of Americana.[25]

In 1926, Phillips Russell, one of the more imaginative of Franklin's biographers, claimed to see evidence that "Polly is mostly Benjamin." Mentioning William Franklin, he asserted: "Polly's defense of herself as the mother of a natural child is in reality Franklin's own defense of himself made for the benefit of those critics in Philadelphia who have been saying nasty things about him." Russell stated erroneously that Franklin published the speech in his *Pennsylvania Gazette*. He said that Franklin himself might have been punished had the Pennsylvania law been enforced, and therefore Franklin "imagines himself facing a court; but he transfers the locale to New England." Russell added that Franklin "is not only unrepentant, but mirthful about his peccadilloes" and through Polly "contends that having

25. Van Doren, *Franklin*, 91-94, discusses the problem of William Franklin's parentage. Franklin told his mother in a letter dated April 12, 1750, that William "is now nineteen years of age"; Smyth, ed., *Writings*, III, 4. Sydney George Fisher, in his *Franklin*, claimed that Franklin also had an illegitimate daughter, who married John Foxcroft, but the evidence is flimsy and Van Doren dismisses the claim.

children, no matter by what means, is 'rather a praiseworthy than a punishable action.' "[26]

In 1929, another lively but not very accurate biographer, Bernard Faÿ, a Frenchman, also linked the speech to the stories whispered about Franklin in Philadelphia. But he added a new element. He said Franklin published the speech in his newspaper "to answer the pleasantries of his Junto friends." The Junto was a weekly mutual-improvement club which Franklin had organized. Monsieur Faÿ, drawing upon sources of information strangely unavailable to others, commented: "By these joking paragraphs, Franklin excused himself of the stories people whispered about him, retained his good footing with his old friends, and kept the Junto alive."[27]

It is reasonable to suppose that Franklin privately read or showed the speech to his fellow club members. But it is harder to believe that he wrote it to defend his own conduct or to confound his critics. If anything, such an attempt might boomerang by simply calling attention to a painful situation. Both Russell and Faÿ felt called upon to guess why Franklin published the piece in the *Pennsylvania Gazette,* when all along they should have known that he did no such thing. As suggested earlier, William's existence may help to explain why Franklin did not publish the speech. But it does not seem a likely motive for the speech itself.

What then was Franklin's "motive"? Was it to promote deism? Polly Baker was ostensibly deistical enough to enrapture Peter Annet. Aside from violating the fornication

26. Russell, *Franklin,* III, 113-14.
27. Faÿ, *Franklin,* 205, 206.

law, she could not imagine what she had done wrong. She asked if it could be a crime—"in the Nature of Things"—to add to the population. In words that sound as though they came straight from the fiery pen of Diderot, she exclaimed, "If you, Gentlemen, must be making Laws, do not turn natural and useful Actions into Crimes, by your Prohibitions."[28]

Now Franklin was a deist. His deism was strongest when he was in his teens, but it is fair to say that he was always deistically inclined. He was not, however, a crusader like Annet. He took particular care, after becoming a grown man, not to offend the orthodox nor undermine their faith.[29] Annet took particular care to offend and undermine. It would be foolish to think that Franklin was seriously trying to promote deism by putting the language of deism into Polly's mouth; his reaction to Annet's treatment of the speech may have been a mixture of amusement and astonishment.

In fact, one can argue that Franklin, by letting Polly talk in this manner and then go on to demand a statue to her memory, was having a little fun at the expense of the dedicated deists. It is conceivable that the satire of the speech was directed both at the orthodox religionists who wished to impose their own moral ideas on others and the unorthodox who were forever appealing to Nature.

Most of all, though, Franklin was having some fun with a current craze in English literature, just as Fielding did in

28. *General Advertiser,* April 15, 1747.

29. Interesting in this connection is the rough draft of a letter Franklin wrote to an unknown person; Smyth, ed., *Writings,* IX, 520-22. Pertinent passages by Franklin on his own unorthodox approach to religion are in *ibid.,* I, 295-97, 324-41, 345-47, II, 214-16, III, 143-46, IV, 11-14, IX, 675-77, X, 83-85.

the early part of his *Joseph Andrews,* a satire on *Pamela*. Drawing on what he knew of fornication trials in New England and possibly remembering Addison's assertion in the *Spectator* that if women were admitted to plead in the courts they would carry the eloquence of the bar to new heights, he proceeded to found the American branch of the seduction school of literature. Characteristically, he did so with tongue in cheek. His contribution was a sort of American "tall story" in which his New England heroine outdid her British cousins in the number of her illegal offspring, in the pain of her public punishment, and in the splendor of her vindication.

Though Franklin wrote the speech more in fun than in protest against orthodox society, he could not foresee the mood of the last half of his century. As men grew more and more impatient with laws imposed by rulers and priests—laws which seemed to sanctify unnatural actions or turn natural actions into crimes—Polly Baker took on a different meaning. As we have seen, she was kidnapped and put to work in France by men who were protesting in earnest. Raynal, Diderot, and Brissot helped themselves to the propaganda inherent in the speech.[30] They suppressed Franklin's humor. They amplified Polly's anguished cry against conventional morality, and she became an intrepid symbol of the revolutionary spirit.

Ironically, there came a black day in 1782, thirty-five years after the appearance of the speech, when Dr. Franklin himself had lost his playful mood. He was in the midst of the tangled, wearisome, discouraging negotiations for a

30. This point is well made by Johansson, *Diderot,* 192.

peace treaty with the British. Only a few weeks before, he
had fabricated his sordid hoax about the scalping of Americans by Indians in the pay of the British, and printed it in
the guise of a *Supplement to the Boston Independent Chronicle*. He longed to escape from the disgust of political
manipulations and return to his beloved scientific experiments. He wrote to Joseph Priestley:

Men I find to be a Sort of Beings very badly constructed,
as they are generally more easily provok'd than reconcil'd,
more disposed to do Mischief to each other than to make
Reparation, much more easily deceiv'd than undeceiv'd,
and having more Pride and even Pleasure in killing than in
begetting one another; for without a Blush they assemble
in great armies at NoonDay to destroy, and when they have
kill'd as many as they can, they exaggerate the Number to
augment the fancied Glory; but they creep into Corners, or
cover themselves with the Darkness of night, when they
mean to beget, as being asham'd of a virtuous Action.[31]

In that moment of unaccustomed bitterness, Benjamin
Franklin may have been closer than ever before to the young
woman whom he had created in jest and who had sur-
prisingly become one of the firebrands of the century.

31. Franklin to Priestley, Passy, June 7, 1782, Smyth, ed., *Writings,* VIII,
451-52.

CHAPTER *Nine*

A Literary Detective Story

INASMUCH as Franklin suppressed Polly Baker in Philadelphia, how did she happen to fly across the Atlantic? How did her speech fall into the competent hands of Henry Woodfall, Jr., and into the columns of his *General Advertiser* in April 1747? This is a mystery story with plenty of suspects.

First, let us consider the possibility that Franklin himself was the agent. He did not leave the Western Hemisphere during the 1730's and 1740's, but he could have sent the manuscript to someone in England. Whom did he know there in 1747? Having worked in two London printing-houses about twenty years before, he may have known Henry Woodfall, Jr., or his elderly father, Henry, Sr., or Wells Egelsham, the journeyman printer whose name appeared in the *General Advertiser* as its ostensible publisher, or someone else employed in the shop. But there is no evidence that he ever wrote to any of them. A more likely suspect would be somebody (1) with whom he corresponded actively; (2) whom he trusted as a friend; and (3) who knew his way around the London printing-houses.

There was a man who met all those requirements very well. His name was William Strahan.

Strahan, then thirty-two years old, was a Scotsman in London who was on his way toward becoming the leading printer and bookseller in England. At that time he and Franklin had not met face to face, but they had been corresponding since 1743 on increasingly friendly terms. Franklin bought books and pamphlets through Strahan and sent him American books and news of the colonies. Later, after Franklin moved to London in 1757, they became close companions, and Strahan printed thirty of Franklin's pseudonymous letters in his tri-weekly paper, the *London Chronicle*. Only one other London newspaper printed more of his letters between 1758 and 1775, and this, strangely enough, was Henry Sampson Woodfall's *Public Advertiser,* the same sheet which, under another name, had introduced Polly's speech in 1747.[1]

We do not know whether Strahan owned stock in the Woodfall paper in 1747, but he did in the 1770's—one twentieth share. He was also partner to Henry Woodfall, Jr., in a law printing business from 1762 until Woodfall's death in 1769.[2] It is difficult to imagine that he was not acquainted with him in 1747, since they were two of the most promising printing-house proprietors in London and must

1. Concerning Strahan and the printing of Franklin's letters in the *London Chronicle* and the *Public Advertiser,* see Crane, *Franklin's Letters to the Press,* xiv-xvi, xxii. Franklin's correspondence with Strahan between 1743 and 1747, obviously incomplete, appears in Smyth, ed., *Writings,* II, 237 and *passim.* Henry Sampson Woodfall was eight years old in 1747.

2. Crane, *Franklin's Letters to the Press,* xxii; [Richard Arthur Austen-Leigh], *The Story of a Printing House, Being a Short Account of the Strahans and Spottiswoodes,* 2nd edn. (London, 1912), 10, 15.

have met in professional and social gatherings of master printers, if nowhere else.

Therefore it is a reasonable guess that Franklin early in 1747 sent a copy of Polly's speech to William Strahan, and that Strahan, having no newspaper of his own at that time, slipped it to Henry Woodfall, Jr., who put it in the *General Advertiser*. Perhaps Franklin wrote Strahan, suggesting that he discreetly insert the piece in a London periodical. Or he may have sent the essay to Strahan without any intention of having it published. In any case no such letter is available today. And we do not know whether that is because Strahan burned it, or because it has been accidentally lost, or because it never existed.

Miss Baker's first transatlantic crossing may indeed have taken place under different auspices. For example, there lived in Philadelphia two other men who could have provided Strahan with a copy of the speech—with or without Franklin's knowledge.

One was David Hall, Franklin's excellent foreman, soon to become his partner. Hall, a Scotsman like Strahan, had worked in Strahan's London printing-house. In 1744, through an arrangement between Strahan and Franklin, he had left Strahan's employ and moved to Philadelphia to enter Franklin's. He was, said Franklin, "obliging, discreet, industrious, and honest."[3]

The other possible source was James Read, a neighbor of Franklin's and a cousin of Franklin's mother-in-law. In 1739, when he was 21 years old, Read had taken a trip to London, where he had made Strahan's acquaintance. If

---

3. Franklin to Strahan, Smyth, ed., *Writings*, II, 243. There, this letter is dated Feb. 12, 1744, but the correct date is believed to be Feb. 12, 1745. Hall did not arrive in Philadelphia until June 1744.

the speech was already in existence at that time, it is just possible, but not very likely, that young "Jemmy" Read took a copy with him. In 1743, when Strahan wished to find a promising American position for David Hall, he wrote to Read in Philadelphia. Read showed the letter to Franklin. Franklin wrote to Strahan, offering to employ Hall, and that was the beginning of a forty-year friendship between Franklin and Strahan. Read, becoming a bookseller, ordered a big consignment of books from Strahan in 1745, and the bill, which came to about £132, required half a century to collect; but the growing unpleasantness over this affair presumably does not rule out the possibility that Read sent the Polly Baker manuscript to Strahan in 1747 or before.[4]

Though William Strahan may be considered the chief suspect as a go-between in the publication of Polly's speech, there are other possibilities. On the English side, a certain Mr. Wygate, or Wigate, an ingenious and well-educated man, had worked side by side with Franklin at Watts's printing-house in 1726. Franklin had taught him to swim and had very nearly decided to travel with him through Europe as an itinerant printer instead of returning to America. In later life he kept in touch with him: for example, Franklin asked Strahan in a letter in 1744 "to remember me affectionately to my old friend Mr. Wigate, to whom I shall write *per* next opportunity."[5]

There was also Peter Collinson, a benevolent cloth merchant and Fellow of the Royal Society, vastly interested

4. For Read's relations with Strahan, see J. Bennett Nolan, *Printer Strahan's Book Account* (Reading, Pa., 1939), especially 6-7, 11-12, 18, 25-27. This book does not mention Polly Baker.

5. Franklin to Strahan, July 4, 1744, Smyth, ed., *Writings,* II, 280. See also Franklin's Autobiography, *ibid.,* I, 284-85.

in scientific advancement and in American affairs. Since 1732, Collinson had been acting as London agent for the Library Company which Franklin and his Junto friends had organized. At the end of March in 1747, less than three weeks before Polly's speech came out in London, Franklin began writing to Collinson a series of remarkable letters on electricity, and it was these letters which Edward Cave printed in pamphlet form in 1751, marking the commencement of Franklin's international fame.[6] Collinson was a Quaker, and perhaps not the man one would choose to publicize a saucy and irreverent maid like Polly. Yet on March 27, 1732, Collinson wrote Thomas Story: "A curious gentleman from Maryland sent me a poem of his own composing which at the request of my intimates was printed here. I doubt not but thee'll find it very entertaining, being interwoven with many diverting incidents and fine reflections." One of the "diverting incidents" involves a Quaker who is not shown in a very favorable light. Since Collinson was capable of having this comical poem printed, perhaps we should not assume that he would have been shocked by the speech of Polly Baker.[7]

As for the American side, it is possible that someone in Franklin's club, the Junto, obtained a copy and sent it to England, with or without Franklin's blessing. One of the rules of the club was that each member, once in three months, must "produce and read an essay of his own writing, on any subject he pleased." Surely Polly's speech must have been either read to the clubmen or passed around

6. Verner W. Crane, *Benjamin Franklin and a Rising People* (Boston, 1954), 33, 48-49, 52-53.

7. Letter from Frederick B. Tolles to the author, Sept. 28, 1955. Mr. Tolles believes that the poem was almost certainly Ebenezer Cook's *Sot-Weed Factor*.

among them. In his autobiography Franklin describes the men who originally made up the Junto in 1727. The one who seems the best suspect is a "good-natur'd, friendly" man, "very ingenious in many little Nicknackeries," named Joseph Breintnall.[8]

Breintnall, like Collinson, was nominally a Quaker but apparently was not always in good standing. A good Quaker named John Smith wrote that he was "remarkable for deistical principles." Breintnall copied deeds for a living, but his interests went much further. In 1729 he teamed with Franklin to write a series of humorous papers, signed "The Busy-Body," in the *American Weekly Mercury* at Philadelphia. That same year he also collaborated with him in experiments to determine the relation of color to heat absorption. In 1735 he sent Peter Collinson a curious account of a rattlesnake and a blacksnake. On February 10, 1746, he addressed another rattlesnake story to Collinson, this time the rattlesnake's victim being Breintnall himself, who described in blood-chilling detail the effects of the bite. His letter was read before the Royal Society and printed in its *Philosophical Transactions,* and the *London Magazine* reprinted it in April 1747, only two pages before the speech of Polly Baker. At least three other British magazines published the rattlesnake story in their April issues. But Breintnall never knew of his literary triumph, for he seems to have survived the snake only to perish by drowning about March 17, 1746, five weeks after he wrote about the snakebite. This means that he could not have sent Polly's outburst to England in 1747, but he could have

8. Smyth, ed., *Writings,* I, 299. The name is there spelled "Breintnal," but it is spelled with two "l's" in his signature in the library of the American Philosophical Society, Franklin Papers, LXIX, 48.

sent it in 1746—perhaps to Collinson—and Collinson could have kept it around for a year or so, like a time bomb, before exploding it in the press.[9]

Junto members were not the only persons who could have handled the Polly manuscript. For example, various printers worked for Franklin for short periods before traveling on. Some of them probably lodged in his house.[10] One or more of them may have seen the speech and even carried copies out of town.

Now, one of the printers who worked in Franklin's shop was a Bostonian named Jonas Green. Moving on to Annapolis, he became the proprietor of the *Maryland Gazette*. The most interesting question about Green is not whether he forwarded the speech to England (though conceivably he might have done so), but whether he procured a copy from Franklin and printed it in his own paper. It will be recalled that Green, in presenting the speech on August 11, 1747, said the British periodicals had printed it incorrectly—"and happening to have a correct Copy of it by me, I cannot think it amiss to give it my Readers."

Green of course did not mention Franklin's name. He presented Polly's defense in a straight-faced manner, as though he possessed an accurate transcript of the courtroom

9. Concerning John Smith, also Breintnall's drowning, see Frederick B. Tolles, "A Note on Joseph Breintnall, Franklin's Collaborator," *Philological Quarterly*, 21 (1942), 247-49. For the "Busy-Body" papers, which started Feb. 4, 1729, see Labaree and Bell, eds., *Papers of Franklin*, I, 113-39. For the scientific collaboration see Crane, *Franklin and a Rising People*, 42. As for the 1735 snake account, see Collinson's reply in the library of the American Philosophical Society, Franklin Papers, LXIX, 48. The 1746 account was read before the Royal Society on April 10, 1746, printed in *Philosophical Transactions*, No. 479 for March and April 1746, and issued again in 1748 as part of Vol. XLIV, Part I, for the year 1746. It is in the April 1747 numbers of the *London Magazine* (16: 176-77), the *Newcastle General Magazine*, the *British Magazine* (Edinburgh), and the *London Magazine* (Dublin).

10. Van Doren, *Franklin*, 125.

proceedings. Thus he aided, abetted, and compounded Franklin's hoax. The mystery, however, is where his version really came from. Had he obtained a copy from Franklin? Or did he simply alter the text which had appeared in the other newspapers and fraudulently represent it as a "correct Copy" in order to puff the importance of his own sheet?

The main distinguishing feature of the *Maryland Gazette* text is a passage of about ninety words which has been quoted earlier. It is a tirade against the fornication law and its "horrid Consequences." The consequences are described in this language: "What Numbers of procur'd Abortions! and how many distress'd Mothers have been driven, by the Terror of Punishment and public Shame, to imbrue, contrary to Nature, their own trembling Hands in the Blood of their helpless Offspring!" Then Polly demands that the law which is guilty of all these "Barbarities and Murders" be repealed and "expung'd for ever from your Books."

This heavy-handed passage does not match the style of the rest of the speech. It introduces an eye-rolling Polly who is just not the same girl Franklin created. It suggests the emotional French phrases which the Abbé Raynal was to put into Polly's mouth twenty-three years later. Therefore one must suspect Mr. Green of inventing the passage. If he did, his choice of language may have been influenced by the tragic death of a young woman in the Annapolis community. Green's own paper, about three months before, had printed several depositions concerning one Mary Freeman, who seems to have stated on her deathbed that a man named John Hance had ruined her, body and soul, forever.[11]

11. *Maryland Gazette*, May 5, 1747.

Though Green must be suspected of a hoax within a hoax, the explanation is not wholly satisfying. After all, he had worked for Franklin about ten years before, and he had continued to have business dealings with him during the 1740's. Not much of their correspondence survives, but Green did write Franklin a friendly and informal letter only seventeen days before printing the Polly Baker story. He sent his hearty respects to Franklin and his wife, "not forgetting Miss Sally."[12] Sally Franklin was not yet four, and if Green had ever seen her, he must have recently revisited Philadelphia. In April, the month when Polly had spoken out in the London press, Franklin had sold sixty reams of paper to Green.[13] In short, Green could have obtained a manuscript copy of one draft of the speech from Franklin.

Besides, the mysterious inserted passage, though uncharacteristic of Polly, contains an expression about imbruing hands in blood which bobs up repeatedly in Franklin's later writings. In 1764, after a gang of unidentified white men had massacred twenty innocent Indians in Pennsylvania, he wrote, "You have imbrued your Hands in innocent Blood; how will you make them clean?" About the same time, he charged that certain pamphlets were instigating the "mad armed Mob . . . to imbrue their Hands in the Blood of their Fellow Citizens." In 1765, at London, he wanted to know if those who wrote against the Americans in the British press "hope to provoke the nation . . . to embrue its hands in the blood of its, perhaps mistaken chil-

12. Reprinted in Lawrence C. Wroth, *A History of Printing in Colonial Maryland, 1686-1776* (Baltimore, 1922), 82-83, citing manuscript in library of American Philosophical Society, Franklin Papers, I, 6. The letter is dated July 25, 1747.

13. George Simpson Eddy, ed., *Account Books Kept by Benjamin Franklin* (New York, 1929), II, 65, 66.

dren?" In 1766 the *Public Advertiser* printed a satirical letter, probably by Franklin; it contained a proposal that an army of Highlanders be sent to America to burn all the capitals of the several provinces and cut the throats of all the inhabitants—but the regular troops quartered there should not be employed in the massacre, "as it is to be feared they would be rather backward in embruing their Hands in the Blood of their Brethren and Fellow Subjects." At least two other times in London, Franklin suggested that certain people would be pleased to have the English imbrue their hands in the blood of the colonists.[14]

None of this proves that Franklin was the author of the extraneous passage. Verner W. Crane, who kindly pointed out these "imbrue-in-blood" examples, commented that the expression was a cliché, and anyone might have used it.[15] When all is considered, however, one cannot feel certain that Franklin did not originate the passage. He was capable of using this sort of language, even with exclamation points, when he was in a pamphleteering mood. Could he have written the passage at a time when he was aroused over some Philadelphia case of infanticide?[16]

Perhaps eventually there will come to light some long-hibernating correspondence between Franklin and Green, solving the mystery of the *Maryland Gazette* account. Up to now, there is no evidence that Franklin ever acknowledged in writing that he was the author of Polly's speech. He may have been cautious on this score for the same

14. The examples are in Smyth, ed., *Writings*, IV, 311, 353-54, VI, 215; and Crane, *Franklin's Letters to the Press*, 42, 56, 66.

15. Letter to the author, May 30, 1956.

16. For other differences between *Maryland Gazette* text and other texts, see Appendix, Comparison of Texts.

reasons which deterred him from publishing the speech itself.

It is possible, however, that there was a further reason, growing more important with the passing years. As Polly Baker's fame spread, New England tended to become unsavory and ridiculous in the eyes of many readers. One writer has said of the speech that "its rapid and popular welcome, both in England and on the Continent, which was like that of 'Gulliver's Travels,' or 'Robinson Crusoe,' soon brought all New England into disrepute in the minds of respectable people."[17] Though this may be an exaggeration, it probably contains a nucleus of truth.

Franklin must have regretted any harm that his wit had inflicted on New England's good name. He bore no bitterness toward the region. In 1755, after revisiting Boston, he wrote to a friend: "I left New England slowly, and with great reluctance. Short day's journeys, and loitering visits on the road, for three or four weeks, manifested my unwillingness to quit a country, in which I drew my first breath, spent my earliest and most pleasant days, and had now received so many fresh marks of the people's goodness and benevolence."[18] During Franklin's long sojourns in London, from 1757 to 1762 and again from 1764 to 1775, he made it his business to put the colonies, including New England, in a favorable light. For example, in 1766, after an English writer had accused the Americans of persecuting old women for witches and being intolerant of other sects, Franklin wrote in the *Gazetteer* that "we were wise enough to leave off both those foolish tricks, long before Old Eng-

17. Arnold, *Historic Side-lights*, 141.
18. Franklin to Catherine Ray, March 4, 1755, Smyth, ed., *Writings*, III, 245.

land made the act of toleration, or repealed the statute against witchcraft."[19]   In 1770, the same year the Abbé Raynal printed the speech of Polly Baker to support his claim that laws too severe still existed in New England, Franklin became the salaried London agent of the Massachusetts House of Representatives and thus gained an additional incentive to remain silent about his authorship. Around 1782, when he was in France, he said in a letter to a man named Stockar that Raynal's *Histoire Philosophique et Politique* was on the whole an excellent work but contained errors.   Among the errors, he listed these statements: "that European Animals degenerate in America.   That men are shorter liv'd.   That they have a bad habit of Inticing Inhabitants.   That the people of Massachusetts Bay preserve their Fanaticism."[20]

By that time Franklin had already told Raynal that Polly was a creature of his own fancy.   But the great man did not unlock the mystery of how the story found its way into print.

19. Crane, *Franklin's Letters to the Press*, 52.
20. Smyth, ed., *Writings*, I, 206.   Smyth implies that Franklin's comments were in response to a letter of Dec. 6, 1781, from one Stockar.   The library of the American Philosophical Society possesses not only this letter from Stockar, but also another dated Aug. 3, 1782, indicating that Franklin had failed to reply to the first, and still another of April 14, 1783, indicating that Franklin had by that time replied.   Stockar was asking Franklin's advice about Raynal's "History of the American Revolution," which was a part of the 1780 edition of the *Histoire* and was also published separately.   Franklin's comments quoted here obviously pertain to the larger work.

CHAPTER *Ten*

Voltaire and Other Debunkers

THE hilarious news that Benjamin Franklin had fathered Polly Baker's speech must have spread rapidly to a good many persons in the salons of Paris. Apparently, the first publication of the news was made in the works of Voltaire.

When John Adams wrote that Franklin's reputation was more universal than Voltaire's, he could hardly have used stronger language. This literary genius, born François Marie Arouet, in 1694, the son of a middle-class Parisian notary, had chosen for himself the name "Monsieur de Voltaire" and made it world famous. As poet, playwright, novelist, historian, and journalist, he spent his long life in combat against injustice, intolerance, and superstition, moving often between France and Switzerland to evade the authorities. In his old age, still battling, he became a legend.[1]

In February 1778, he returned to Paris after an absence of twenty-eight years, and was strenuously acclaimed. Franklin was already there, being idolized—his portrait hanging over Parisian mantelpieces, his likeness on medal-

1. André Maurois, "Voltaire," in *French Thought in the Eighteenth Century,* 133-36.

lions and snuffboxes everywhere. When the two heroes met, excitement swept the city. Voltaire and Franklin had expressed admiration for each other in their writings, and Voltaire had once erected a lightning conductor in Franklin's honor.[2] Now they came face to face. The first meeting was in Voltaire's quarters. Voltaire was eighty-three, Franklin seventy-two. With the American was Temple Franklin, his eighteen-year-old grandson. Franklin requested a benediction. The Frenchman laid his hand on the youth's head and solemnly said in English, "God and Liberty." He added that this was the only benediction that suited the grandson of Monsieur Franklin. Voltaire reported later that "all who were present shed tears of tenderness." Franklin and Voltaire also saw each other at a Masonic lodge ceremony. But the most celebrated meeting took place at a public session of the Academy of Sciences on April 29. The audience insisted that the two men be introduced to each other. They bowed, spoke, and then grasped hands, but the clamor continued and would not subside until they had embraced in the French manner and kissed each other's cheeks. The word spread throughout the kingdom that "Solon and Sophocles" had embraced.[3] Voltaire died one month later; Franklin lived on for twelve more useful years.

One of Voltaire's major works was his *Dictionnaire Philosophique* ("Philosophical Dictionary"). From time to

2. Voltaire to A. M. Marriott, Feb, 26, 1767, *Oeuvres Complètes de Voltaire* (Paris, 1877-1885), XLV, 137; Franklin to Henry Bouquet, Sept. 30, 1764, Smyth, ed., *Writings,* IV, 267-68. For the lightning conductor see M. de Saussure to Franklin, Feb. 23, 1773, *ibid.,* I, 104.

3. Account of the Franklin-Voltaire meetings is in Van Doren, *Franklin,* 605-6, and Parton, *Franklin,* II, 315-17. See also Marquis de Condorcet, *Vie de Voltaire,* in *Oeuvres Complètes de Voltaire* (Kehl edn., 1784-1789), LXX, 152-53.

time, during the last twenty-five years of his life, he wrote brief articles with such titles as "Abraham," "Destiny," "Man," "Miracles," and "Religion" and published them in alphabetical order, edition following edition in rapid succession. At a time when the expanding collection was being published under the title *Questions sur l'Encyclopédie par des Amateurs* ("Questions on the Encyclopaedia by Enthusiasts"),[4] Voltaire included an exposé of certain fictitious anecdotes which had been used as historical facts. And into this exposé, in 1774, he inserted a passage about the anecdotes in the Abbé Raynal's *Histoire Philosophique et Politique.* He ended the insertion by commenting, "How many tales have embellished and disfigured every history."[5]

In this passage Voltaire did not mention the speech of Polly Baker. But after his death in 1778 a great edition of his works was assembled at Kehl, Germany, and published in seventy volumes between 1784 and 1789. The editors, who included the dramatist Beaumarchais and the philosopher Condorcet, put into it much new matter which they had found among Voltaire's papers.[6] All the alphabetical articles which had been published in various editions were combined under the title *Dictionnaire Philosophique,* occupying seven volumes. And in the article headed "ANA, ANECDOTES," immediately preceding the sentence, "How

4. Louis Du Bois, "Notice sur le Dictionnaire Philosophique," in *Oeuvres de Voltaire* (Paris, 1826), LI, ii; Bernard Gagnebin's introduction to *Voltaire: Lettres Inédites à Son Imprimeur* (Genève, 1952), xviii, xxxix; Georges Bengesco, *Voltaire: Bibliographie de Ses Oeuvres* (Paris, 1882), I, 422-23.

5. From *Questions sur l'Encyclopédie par des Amateurs* as it appeared in *Oeuvres de Mr de Voltaire* (1775), XXV, 191. A note on the passage is in Feugère, *Raynal*, 219n.

6. See "De l'Imprimerie de la Société Littéraire-Typographie," *Oeuvres de Voltaire* (Kehl edn.), I, viii. Apparently this volume was first published in 1784. The copy I consulted is dated 1785.

many tales have embellished and disfigured every history," appeared a new comment on Raynal's *Histoire*: "The speech of a woman of Boston to her judges who were condemning her to punishment for the fifth time, because she had brought to bed a fifth child, is a joke, a lampoon of the illustrious Franklin, and it is related in the same work as an authentic piece."[7]

In the absence of contrary evidence, it is reasonable to conclude that Voltaire wrote this passage at Paris during the four final hectic months of his life and left it among his papers—and that his source was probably the illustrious Franklin himself.[8]

Voltaire's expressions are worth noting. He says "Boston," whereas Raynal had been no more specific than "New England." He uses the French word *pamphlet,* which can mean in English either "pamphlet" or "lampoon," and he does not say that the speech was written for a newspaper.

In the final volume of the Kehl edition, there is a biography of Voltaire, by Condorcet. Describing the famous meetings of Voltaire and Franklin in 1778, Condorcet remarked that Franklin, like Voltaire, had often used the weapon of the joke which corrects human folly.[9] Doubtless the story of Polly Baker was one of the jokes that Condorcet had in mind.

When Voltaire's reference to Polly appeared in print, Franklin still had more than four years to live. During those

7. *Ibid.,* XXXVII, 277-78.

8. One cannot be positive that the sentence was written by Voltaire, since it would have been possible for one of the editors at Kehl to have composed and inserted it, but there seems to be no reason to treat this possibility as anything more than remote. Voltaire was forever revising and enlarging his alphabetical writings.

9. *Oeuvres de Voltaire* (Kehl edn.), LXX, 152.

years another writer published the information that Franklin was Polly's creator. This was Philip Mazzei, an Italian who had spent six of his most active years in Virginia.

Born of bourgeois stock near Florence in 1730, Mazzei became a physician, a horticulturist, and an enthusiast for everything American. His interest in America was stimulated by Franklin, whom he met in England. In 1773 he established himself—also the grape and the olive—on Virginia soil and became a lifelong friend of Thomas Jefferson. He helped Jefferson in the battle for religious freedom in Virginia. Jefferson once spoke of him as "possessed of a masculine understanding," but on another occasion described him as a man likely to "over act his part." In 1779, Governor Patrick Henry sent Mazzei to Europe in the hope that he could persuade the Grand-Duke of Tuscany to lend money to Virginia. At Paris, Mazzei promptly had a disagreement with Franklin, who strongly believed that foreign affairs should be left to Congress and that Virginia had no business sending its own representative. Mazzei accomplished little and blamed Franklin for his failure. He finally returned to Virginia, but in 1785 was back in Paris on his own, deplorably short of funds.[10]

Mazzei's financial plight coincided with a seizure of indignation over the inaccurate writings of two Frenchmen, the Abbé Mably and the Abbé Raynal, concerning American affairs. So he determined to refute the Abbés and fatten his

10. Richard Cecil Garlick, Jr., *Philip Mazzei, Friend of Jefferson* (Baltimore, 1933), especially 9, 39, 61-73, 164-65; and Philip Mazzei, *Memoirs of the Life and Peregrinations of the Florentine Philip Mazzei, 1730-1816,* trans. Howard R. Marraro (New York, 1942), 173, 188, 245-47. The quotations from Jefferson are in Garlick, p. 165.

purse by writing a book. With the help of Jefferson, who was then the United States minister to France, he did so. He wrote the book in Italian and had it translated into French before publication. It appeared in 1788 in four volumes, under the title *Recherches Historiques et Politiques sur les États-Unis de l'Amérique Septentrionale* ("Historical and Political Researches on the United States of North America"). The author's name was not given—only "By a citizen of Virginia." Jefferson considered the book "very good." Mazzei's biographer, Richard Cecil Garlick, Jr., calls it "the first accurate history of the American colonies in French."[11]

In his third volume Mazzei mercilessly bombarded the American portions of Raynal's celebrated *Histoire.* And one of his special targets was Raynal's use of the speech of Polly Baker. As proof that the episode was spurious, Mazzei described the same conversation among Franklin, Silas Deane, and Raynal which Jefferson put in writing many years later. His account is remarkably like Jefferson's, though with certain minor differences. Jefferson does not date the conversation, but Mazzei says it took place toward the end of 1777 or at the beginning of 1778. Mazzei omits the erroneous statement which Jefferson attributes to Deane: "I know there never was such a law in Massachusets." Like Jefferson, however, he puts into Franklin's mouth the statement that when he was printing a newspaper it sometimes happened that he lacked materials to fill the sheet and amused himself by making up tales, "and this of Polly Baker is of that number." The anecdote ends with the

11. Garlick, *Mazzei*, 100-14; Mazzei's *Memoirs*, 295-97.

same sort of remark on the part of Raynal that Jefferson relates: "My word, I am more pleased to have put in my book your tales than other men's truths."[12]

In fact, it seems probable that Mazzei learned of this conversation from Jefferson himself and published it with his approval.[13]

Jefferson may also have approved some of Mazzei's further observations about Raynal and Polly. The Italian severely criticizes Raynal for not making an "honest retreat" in the 1780 edition of the *Histoire*. He says Raynal ought to have either suppressed the speech or added a note explaining that it was an ingenious satire composed by Franklin in the manner of great men who endeavor to render useful even that which they do for their own amusement. Raynal, in Mazzei's opinion, could have informed his readers that the strictness which still existed in New England when he published the first edition of his work had at last been forced—thanks to the American Revolution —to make way for a reasonable indulgence. Mazzei also chides Raynal for saying of Polly's speech, "So superior is the voice of reason to all the powers of studied eloquence." In this, says Mazzei, the Frenchman "does too much honor to our poor American girls in supposing that they talk the way the Doctor writes."[14]

12. [Mazzei], *Recherches Historiques et Politiques*, III, 23-24.

13. Johansson, *Diderot*, 162-63, concludes that Mazzei probably received the anecdote from Jefferson, and the circumstances support the conclusion. As we have already seen, the anecdote in its surviving form contains factual errors, but there is no special reason to doubt the accuracy of Jefferson's recollection that he heard such a story from Franklin in Paris—that is, in 1784 or 1785. Garlick, *Mazzei*, 100-4, tells how Jefferson provided facts and opinions to Mazzei for his book.

14. Mazzei, *Recherches Historiques et Politiques*, III, 24-25.

Raynal did indeed have the opportunity of making an honest retreat, if Mazzei was correct that Raynal learned about Polly's origin in 1777 or 1778. Perhaps he simply could not bring himself to sacrifice, for the sake of mere truth, one of the most intriguing episodes in his profitable book. Polly continued to pose as a historical figure, not only in the 1780 edition, but also in a new one published in 1820, long after the author had left the field of contention.

By that time the speech had been debunked time and again. J. P. Brissot de Warville, one of the Frenchmen who had reprinted Polly's speech, made an American trip in 1788 and published an account of it three years later during the French Revolution.[15] This book was translated into English by Joel Barlow of Connecticut and published in 1792 in London, Dublin, and New York. At one point the translator, disapproving something Brissot had written about American agriculture, said in a footnote: "Accounts like this put one in mind of Dr. Franklin's romance of *Mary Baker,* so religiously believed and copied by the Abbé Raynal, in his History of the Two Indies."[16] There are two curious facts about this comment. One is that Polly again is called "Mary Baker." The other is that Joel Barlow did not know, or at least did not bring out, that Brissot himself, as well as Raynal, had fallen for Franklin's hoax.

In 1813 a French gentleman whose name was Egide Louis Edmé Joseph de l'Espinasse, Chevalier de Langeac,

15. Brissot de Warville, *Nouveau Voyage dans les États-Unis de l'Amérique septentrionale* (3 vols., Paris, 1791).

16. J. P. Brissot de Warville, *New Travels in the United States of America.* In the London and Dublin editions, see p. 331; in the New York edition, see p. 182. The translator's name is not given, but Ellery, *Brissot,* 479, says that Barlow was the translator, and so does the Library of Congress catalogue.

published an anonymous work entitled *Anecdotes Anglaises et Américaines* ("English and American Anecdotes"). He squeezed two choice anecdotes out of the affair of "Polly-Baker." First, he slyly recited the speech itself (incidentally placing it in the "county of Connecticut" during the American Revolutionary War). Then he gleefully presented the story of how Franklin deprived Raynal of his illusions about the speech. This story he apparently took from Mazzei's book of twenty-five years earlier. Langeac added his own scornful comment about the Abbé Raynal: "There you see how this *philosophe* wrote history."[17]

It was now time for another debunking in English. A British army officer, Lieutenant Francis Hall of the 14th Light Dragoons, toured North America and wrote a book entitled *Travels in Canada, and the United States, in 1816 and 1817.* It was published in London in 1818 and was promptly reprinted in Boston. It must have met with a good reception among the English, for a second London edition appeared in 1819. The author reported many interesting details, including the astonishing size of the men from west of the Appalachians whom he saw in the weekly "drawing-rooms" at the White House and whose stature, he said, was "certainly a considerable stumbling-block to the Abbé Raynal's theory" that the Americans were deteriorating. In Utica, New York, he noted a tobacconist's sign on which were three grim faces and these lines:

17. *Anecdotes* (Paris, 1813), II, 130-39. Langeac used the same French translation of Polly's speech that had appeared in *Courier de l'Europe* and *Courier Politique et Littéraire* on June 17, 1777, the only substantial differences being in the last few sentences. Those differences, however, suggest that he may have copied the speech from some intermediate printing, for they are changes that Langeac had no apparent reason to make.

We three are engag'd in one cause;
I snuffs, I smokes, and I chaws.

And while traveling through Virginia in January 1817 he had the honor of spending a day at Jefferson's home, Monticello. From the former president, then in his seventies, came an unabated flow of conversation, and one of the stories he told his visitor was the anecdote of Raynal's visit to Franklin's house in Passy. The lieutenant recorded the story in his book, commenting that it "serves to show how history, even when it calls itself philosophical, is written."

This version does not name Silas Deane. Hall quotes Jefferson as merely saying that "one of the company observed, that no such law as that alluded to in the story, existed in New England." Franklin's disclosure is given in these words: "I can account for all this; you took the anecdote from a newspaper, of which I was at that time editor, and, happening to be very short of news, I composed and inserted the whole story." Raynal then makes the same graceful retreat as in the other versions.[18]

Soon Jefferson provided his own written account of the episode. He received a letter from a man named Robert Walsh, asking some questions about Franklin, and on December 4, 1818, Jefferson sent him seven anecdotes, all of which have become precious bits of Frankliniana. One was the conversation among Franklin, Deane, and Raynal.

In 1827 the Franklin-Raynal anecdote again made an appearance in England, this time in a periodical called *The Table Book,* published by William Hone. Instead of taking the yarn from Francis Hall's *Travels,* however, Hone

18. Hall, *Travels* (Boston, 1818), 200, 111, 229-30.

apparently translated it from the Chevalier de Langeac, who had probably copied it from Philip Mazzei, who very likely had heard the story from Jefferson. In repeating the tale Hone suppressed Raynal's final remark that he would rather print Franklin's stories than other men's truths. The Englishman evidently did not want to give the Frenchman the last word.[19]

Still another who exposed Polly was Honoré de Balzac. In his novel entitled *A Distinguished Provincial in Paris,* published in 1839, he caused a character to say that Franklin had acknowledged the fraud in the home of Jacques Necker, a French government official.[20] Franklin may indeed have done so, but there is no evidence that Balzac's account is factual.

In 1854, more than a century after Polly's trial was first reported in the British press, Jefferson's anecdote, as sent to Robert Walsh in 1818, found its way into a collection of Jefferson's writings edited by Henry Augustine Washington.[21] After that, the biographers of Benjamin Franklin finally recognized the speech of Polly Baker as one of his products.

A good story dies hard. And even while Voltaire, Mazzei, Joel Barlow, the Chevalier de Langeac, Lieutenant Hall, William Hone, Balzac, and Jefferson were debunking Polly, her words still rang defiantly through the pages of history.

19. *The Table Book* (London), 1 (1827), 89.
20. Balzac, *A Distinguished Provincial in Paris,* trans. Ellen Marriage (Illustrated Library Edition of Balzac's Works, Boston and New York, no date, VIII), 209-10.
21. Washington, *Writings of Jefferson,* VIII, 501-2.

CHAPTER *Eleven*

Polly the Indestructible

A T eight o'clock in the morning of Tuesday, August 9, 1785, somewhere between the Azores and the Madeira Islands, an infirm old man—or perhaps his grandnephew acting for him—leaned over the rail of a ship and took the temperature of the Atlantic Ocean. The water was seventy-three degrees. The air was also seventy-three. The wind came from the northeast. The ship's course was approximately west southwest. Benjamin Franklin was making his last voyage home. That evening at six o'clock the thermometer registered seventy-three in the water and seventy-four in the air.[1] And on the same day, in Springfield, Massachusetts, the *Hampshire Herald* printed the speech of Polly Baker with no mention whatever of Franklin's authorship.[2]

John Russell, the printer and publisher of this newspaper, prefaced the item with these prudential words: *"The*

1. "A Journal of a Voyage from the Channel between France and England towards America in 1785," kept for Franklin by his grandnephew, Jonathan Williams, Jr., Smyth, ed., *Writings*, IX, 410-13. Williams later became the first superintendent of West Point; see Van Doren, *Franklin*, 601.
2. *The Hampshire Herald: or, the Weekly Advertiser*, Aug. 9, 1785. Whitfield J. Bell, Jr., pointed out the presence of the speech in this paper. The text does not differ importantly from that of the English periodicals of 1747.

following is published by particular desire, not with a view of countenancing deviations from the path of virtue, but as a curious singularity."

The Massachusetts paper repeated the familiar statement that the trial had taken place in Connecticut. About nine months later, however, a Connecticut periodical served up the speech with no reference to Connecticut at all, placing the incident vaguely "in New-England." Polly's appearance in the *New-Haven Gazette, and the Connecticut Magazine* on April 27, 1786, was apparently her earliest publicity in the province generally supposed to have been her home, though it is hard to be sure about such things, since no one can pretend to have seen all of the many printings of the speech. The *New-Haven Gazette,* like the *Hampshire Herald,* did not name the illustrious author.[3]

But it was in Franklin's own Philadelphia that the most interesting American revival of Polly Baker took place. In that city, at the beginning of 1787, a newspaper editor named Mathew Carey founded a monthly periodical called the *American Museum.* It became popular and successful. Frank Luther Mott calls Carey the ablest magazine editor of his time in the United States and says the *American Museum* was probably the most important repository of political and economic papers among American magazines of the eighteenth century.[4] In the third issue, dated March 1787, Carey printed Polly's famous plea with no hint of its

3. Jack C. Barnes called attention to the speech in the *New-Haven Gazette, and the Connecticut Magazine,* 1 (April 27, 1786), 86-87. The text is not clearly traceable to any single previous version, but it is bibliographically significant as the propable source of the version presented 78 years later by James Parton in his *Franklin,* I, 219-21.

4. Frank Luther Mott, *American Journalism* (New York, 1942), 139.

authorship and no indication that it was anything but a genuine speech in a Connecticut courtroom.[5]

Carey's straightforward presentation provides us with one of the most intriguing episodes in the long history of Polly's career. Franklin was in Philadelphia at the time. Furthermore he and Carey knew each other very well. For a period of some months Carey had worked for Franklin in France, operating a private press which Franklin had set up to print official documents and for his own amusement.[6] And Franklin had a part in Carey's decision to start the *American Museum*. Both of them thought such a magazine would be useful in preserving "fugitive pieces"—that is, interesting documents that might otherwise disappear into oblivion—and Franklin watched for such pieces and sent them to Carey.[7] Indeed, a notable feature of the *American Museum* was that it published a number of Franklin's own writings. For all these reasons it seems possible that Carey published Polly's speech with Franklin's knowledge.[8]

In 1787 Franklin was eighty-one years old, holding the office of president of Pennsylvania, revered, wealthy, suffering from a stone in the bladder, but generally, Carl Van Doren tells us, "content and cheerfully occupied." In Van

5. *American Museum,* 1 (March 1787), 243-45. In a 3rd edn. of the March number, dated 1792, the speech is at 212-14.
6. Van Doren, *Franklin,* 769.
7. Mathew Carey, *American Museum,* 1 (1787), preface dated Jan. 31, 1787; and Franklin to Carey, June 10, 1788, Smyth, ed., *Writings,* IX, 660-61. Also see *ibid.,* III, 226-27.
8. Possible, though far from certain. On this question Carl Van Doren told the writer in a letter dated May 11, 1950: "Since Carey had worked for Franklin at Passy, and was well known to him, and obviously had his permission to print or reprint other writings of Franklin during these final years 1787-1790, I cannot help supposing that Franklin saw the *Museum* text [of Polly's speech] and may have made some of the changes that differentiate it from other texts. I do not know, for I find no other record of Carey's use of it or any correspondence with Franklin on the subject."

Doren's biography we glimpse the venerable doctor writing at his desk; regaling guests with lively scientific talk under a mulberry tree in his garden; reaching for a book on a high shelf with a long-armed contraption of his own invention; exercising with a dumbbell; relieving his ailment by long hot baths in a copper tub shaped like a shoe, with an open book fixed on the "instep"; riding through the streets in a specially built sedan chair to preside over Pennsylvania's supreme executive council. (Both riding in carriages and walking were painful, and he wished he had a balloon sufficiently large to raise him from the ground, so that a man striding along the street could lead him by a string.) In March he was supervising the completion of additions to his home—a library to house the largest and best private collection of books in America and a dining room seating twenty-four persons, in which George Washington was to have dinner on June 6. When the *American Museum* printed Polly's speech, Philadelphia was preparing for the Constitutional Convention, in which Franklin and Washington were to be the great conciliators without whom the convention might have collapsed.[9]

Mathew Carey, with or without Franklin's blessing, used a text of Polly Baker's speech that did not greatly differ from that of the *Gentleman's Magazine* in 1747. The differences of punctuation are numerous, but there are only trivial changes in the language. In the explanatory words that go with the speech, however, Carey introduces some new thoughts. He adds a note at the end which assures the reader that after Polly married one of her judges she "supported an irreproachable character"—an expression

9. Van Doren, *Franklin*, 736-51.

which appears in no other version. Like the *Gentleman's Magazine,* he says she had fifteen children by her husband. Then he concludes with a startling statement: "N. B. Another account says her name was Sarah Olitor."

What could this mean? Did Franklin provide the name "Sarah Olitor" to Mathew Carey? If so, was it only a further piece of fiction, a prolongation of the joke? The Court of Common Pleas of Hartford County, Connecticut, at some time between 1722 and 1725, sentenced a fornicator named Sarah, but her last name looks more like Colofor than Olitor. In New London County, Connecticut, between 1711 and 1715, a woman described only as "Sarah [——], wife of Isaac Williams," had a child begot before marriage by fornication with Walter Palmer. At Boston, Massachusetts, on January 4, 1709, with Paul Dudley on the Suffolk County panel of justices, a woman named Sarah Oliver was discharged by the court, but the records do not say what she was accused of. At one place her name looks like Olivor, but even that is not quite Olitor.[10] In fact, no Olitors at all can be found, and the only promising discovery is that *olitor* is a Latin word meaning "kitchen gardener"—a person who grows potherbs. Perhaps that was the comical origin of the note in the *American Museum.*

Sarah Olitor remains the most mysterious mystery woman of the affair of Benjamin Franklin and Polly Baker.

The *American Museum,* like other monthly magazines of that century, was reissued in book form. Volume I, cover-

10. Records, Court of Common Pleas, County of Hartford, 1722-1725 (Connecticut State Library, Hartford), about 15 pages from end; New London County Record of Trials, VIII, 67, 101-2 (Connecticut State Library, Hartford); Records of the Court of General Sessions of the Peace, 1702-1712, 181, 1725-1732, 173 (Suffolk County Courthouse, Boston).

ing the first half of 1787 and published that same year, evidently sold briskly, for some of the copies now in libraries contain second or third editions of the monthly numbers. As for the March number, Carey printed a second edition of it later in 1787 and a third in 1792.[11] Thus, despite the debunking which was well underway in Paris, the words of Polly Baker, or Sarah Olitor, continued to reach new readers in the newly established United States of America as the eighteenth century moved toward its end.

Franklin had died in 1790. In 1798 his beloved city witnessed the appearance of a periodical named the *Philadelphia Monthly Magazine*. No one will be astonished to learn that the June issue contained the plea of Polly Baker, evidently reprinted from the *American Museum,* and ending with the same note: "Another account says her name was Sarah Olitor."

The American revival of the speech in the 1780's and 1790's, forty or more years after its original publication, came during an American literary craze for sentimental stories about seduction in the manner of Samuel Richardson's *Pamela* and *Clarissa*. A scholar investigating this Richardsonian vogue once made a study of a representative periodical, the *Massachusetts Magazine,* from 1789 to 1796, and found its fiction characterized by an "appalling interest in themes of seduction and resultant misery." He counted seventy-six of these sad fictional narratives, "to which must be added almost as many more moral essays which have as

---

11. The third edn. is dated 1792, though the January number of the volume in which it is bound in the Harvard College Library is dated 1790 (also a third edn.). In the third edn., the text of Polly's speech is slightly different from that of the first and second edns.

their subject the melancholy effects of seduction!"[12]   Miss Baker does not seem to be among the fallen women in this periodical; perhaps she disqualified herself by finding a happy ending.

It must be considered more than a coincidence that the speech of Polly Baker first appeared in England on the crest of a literary fad on behalf of poor young women endeavoring successfully or unsuccessfully to preserve their virtue; that the speech became popular in France after the Richardsonian influence had leapt the Channel and stirred the tender sentiments of Frenchmen like Diderot; and that it enjoyed a revival in post-Revolutionary America at a time when Richardsonian sentimentality had permeated the fiction of the infant republic.

Meanwhile across the ocean Polly, far from being recognized as fictitious (despite debunking), had been rediscovered and was now assuming new dimensions as a historical figure.   In 1794 a biographical notice appeared in Great Britain, and it contained details of her career which had never before been revealed.   This sketch was entitled "Interesting Reflections on the Life of Miss Polly Baker."   It shows signs of having been written in London and may have first been published in some periodical there.   At any rate it was printed in the April 1794 number of the *Edinburgh Magazine, or Literary Miscellany*.[13]   It began thus:

12. Herbert R. Brown, "Richardson and Sterne in the *Massachusetts Magazine*," *New England Quarterly*, 5 (1932), 71.

13. The *Edinburgh Magazine, or Literary Miscellany*, New Ser., 3 (April 1794), 288-94.   This magazine should not be confused with the *Edinburgh Magazine, and Literary Miscellany*.   I am indebted to Jack F. Kottemann of the Harvard College Library for obligingly searching for this article in the *Edinburgh Magazine, and Literary Miscellany*; and to T. M. Hodges, Reference Librarian at Hamilton College, for locating the article in the other *Edinburgh Magazine* and sending photocopies.   Though the article is in the first person, the author is not named.

"Miss Baker was a beautiful, but unfortunate young woman, of Connecticut, in New England; and daughter of a reputable mechanic, soberly, and, as is the custom of that town, religiously brought up; educated, according to her rank in life, in reading, writing, and plain work, and what is of more consequence, was taken home early from the day school, to be instructed in the useful and domestic duties of life."

Having disposed quickly of Polly's education, the unknown author launched into her love life in paragraphs that are worth quoting in full, for he seems to have ferreted out sources of information that even Franklin did not possess.

She had given early proofs of a masculine understanding, and united with it, what is not often united, that female grace and captivating softness of manners, "in which the charm of woman principally consists."

It was her fate, or rather her misfortune, to form an acquaintance with an agreeable young man, the son of one of the principal magistrates of the town.

An intimacy quickly followed, and few of my readers between eighteen and six and thirty need be told, how soon such an intercourse grows to a tender attachment, and takes a softer name.

They experienced the usual difficulties of love, which are always increased by inequality of condition.

I will not describe the irritated pride and selfish resentment of his parents, or the tender anxieties of hers: anxieties, augmented by their discovering too late, that her affections were fixed on one, whose family would never consent to their union, and whose character was too well known, and his passions too violent to render him at all scrupulous, as to the manner in which he gratified them.

The repeated injunctions and remonstrances of their families, only served to make the young people more diligent in procuring interviews, and to enhance the value of those precious moments, when procured.

It is not my business to dwell on scenes passed over in rapture, but remembered with regret; which, to those best acquainted with them, only prove, that men are false, and women credulous. She was thrown off her guard by his promising to marry her, and in a fatal, incautious moment, undone. Rejected by her relations, perfidiously forsaken by her betrayer, pregnant, without fame, and without a friend, the pains of child-birth were added to wretchedness and loss of reputation;—"and hissing infamy proclaim'd the rest!"

As she recovered, those who had supported her became clamorous in their demands; and her personal beauty being unimpaired, she attracted the loose desires of a neighbouring trader. It has been said, that we are never so far from mis-conduct, as when we start at the shadow of indecorum: and surely the barriers of female modesty cannot be too strictly guarded: for the crouded capital, and the sequestered village, alike shock us with numerous instances of the rapid progress from virgin innocence to undaunted turpitude.

This unhappy woman, so lately the darling of her family, doated on by a lover, who, had *she* been *cruel,* still would have been *kind,* looked up to, and respected for virtue and good sense by all her acquaintance, was now an outcast from society, the ridicule and contempt of many with less virtue, but more prudence than herself; reduced, by a strange kind of base necessity, to support herself and a helpless infant by illicit practices, and to tread the odious and disgusting path of filthy infamy.

The glow of revolting virtue gradually forsook her cheek, and she, who, a few months before, would have revolted at an indelicate allusion, now entered the noisome caves of prostitution, without a blush.

But such conduct was not at that time to be passed over without legal punishment, in New England, which has been called the Land of Saints, the Hot-house of Calvinistic Puritanism.

In consequence of this, and other natural children, she several times suffered whipping, fine, and imprisonment.

On one of these occasions being brought before a court of justice, in order that sentence might be pronounced against her, she craved indulgence of the bench to speak a few words, and surprised her hearers, by the following address, which was taken down in short hand by a person on the spot:—

Here the speech is presented almost in full, some of it quoted as printed in the British press nearly fifty years before, but most of it paraphrased. The text has the appearance of a translation from a foreign language; yet it also looks as though the translator had mixed it with the English original. Polly's closing statement that she deserved a statue to her memory was omitted in the manner of Raynal and Diderot. The author of the "Interesting Reflections" then resumed: "Her judges, as well as all that were present, were moved by the affecting circumstances of her case.—She was discharged without punishment, and a handsome collection directly made for her in court. The public became interested in her behalf; and her original seducer, either from compunction, or from the latent seeds of an affection, which had been suppressed, but never eradicated, married her shortly after."

A striking feature of this 1794 narrative is that Polly became the wife, not of one of her judges, but of her original seducer. That also was the way Denis Diderot had told it in his account of Polly Baker, written about 1780 but not published until the twentieth century. Could the author of the "Interesting Reflections" have examined a manuscript of Diderot's story? If not, both men may have seen some earlier version which is missing today. Or perhaps their imaginations simply chose the same solution to Polly's troubles; certainly their denouement was more conventional than Franklin's. In any case, they did not take the same moral approach. Diderot's sympathies lay clearly with unfortunate women and against all seducers. The author of the "Interesting Reflections" added about two thousand words of moralizing aimed at girls and their parents. He said that although Miss Baker was at last married to her original lover, he trusted that "no woman of common sense will be induced by this rare instance of tardy justice, to imitate *her* misconduct." He created a purple picture of the vulgar and "stupidly gay" prostitutes in the streets of London. True, he did not whitewash the male sex, but he put in a word of praise for a certain Mr. Beckford, who had indulged his amorous nature, "it must be confessed," with "an unbounded and culpable latitude" but had followed an invariable rule "to make an ample provision for his natural children, as well as their mother." And he concluded the essay by quoting one gentleman's explanation of his moral code:

In all my warfare with women (said this person) I never considered myself as justified either to use violent force, intoxicating drugs, or to delude them by promising marriage, or by a mock representation of the ceremony.

It is a serious affair, and not to be trifled with; nor is it a fair proceeding.—If I could work on their vanity, their passions, their hopes, and their fears, it was fair fighting on equal ground; but having recourse to the modes above mentioned, is like fighting with infected weapons, or poisoning the wells and springs of a garrison or country, and contrary to the laws of war.

Nine months after the Edinburgh appearance of "Interesting Reflections on the Life of Miss Polly Baker," the entire piece was reproduced in America. The *New-York Magazine* printed it in January 1795, with credit to the *Edinburgh Magazine*.[14]

What is more, the essay, or rather the first half of it, found its way between the hard covers of a book of biographical sketches. This book, published in London in 1803, bore the title *Eccentric Biography; or, Memoirs of Remarkable Female Characters, Ancient and Modern.* The title page advertised that the subjects included actresses, adventurers, authoresses, fortunetellers, gypsies, dwarfs, swindlers, vagrants, "and others who have distinguished themselves by their Chastity, Dissipation, Intrepidity, Learn-

14. Jack C. Barnes of the University of Maryland pointed out that the "Interesting Reflections" appeared in the *New-York Magazine, or, Literary Repository,* 6 (January 1795), 39-46. This information led to the finding of the piece in the *Edinburgh Magazine.*

ing, Abstinence, Credulity, &c. &c." Among the women so honored were Joan of Arc, Madame du Barry, Catherine I, Catherine II, Lady Godiva, Mary Queen of Scots—and Polly Baker, who was now moving in pretty fast company.

All the newly discovered facts about Polly's life thus gained a further stamp of authenticity. It was repeated that she was the daughter of a reputable mechanic, that her seducer was the son of a magistrate, that she later became the mistress of a trader, that her speech was taken down in shorthand, that a collection was made for her in court, and that her original seducer married her.[15] But the editor of the book, whose name was not given, cut out Polly's reference to the Biblical command, "increase and multiply," explaining that he thought it proper to omit her "specious" arguments concerning religion. He also dropped most of the general comments on morals that had been a part of the "Interesting Reflections."

Now once again the account of Polly's career jumped the Atlantic. In 1804 an American edition of *Eccentric Biography* was issued at Worcester, Massachusetts, by Isaiah Thomas, perhaps the leading publisher of his time in the United States. The book presumably appealed to American readers, because Thomas brought out still another edition in 1805.

Thus we see that the close of the eighteenth century did not by any means signal the eclipse of the young woman who had symbolized the century's enthusiasm for nature's laws. Indeed, ten years after her life story first appeared in a book of biographies, her fame got an even more important boost. The *American Law Journal,* a publication

15. *Eccentric Biography,* 11-16.

crammed with legal documents, including decisions of the
United States Supreme Court, solemnly printed her speech
as though it were an authentic case from the Connecticut
courts.[16]

The *American Law Journal* was published by John E.
Hall. His principal base was Philadelphia, but the bound
volume for 1813, in which Polly appears, indicates that he
was operating that year in Baltimore. A table of contents
in this volume contains the line: "Speech of Miss Polly
Baker. *Bastardy*. . . . 458." The only heading on the
speech is: "SPEECH OF MISS POLLY BAKER, *Delivered
before a Court of Judicature in Connecticut, New England,
where she was prosecuted for having a bastard child.*"
Nothing is added at the end of the discourse; nothing is
said about the verdict of the judges or of Polly's marriage;
and no date is given for the trial. A reader of the *Journal*
might well have assumed that the affair was recent. In fact,
a slight alteration in the text had the effect of lifting the
case out of the colonial era and placing it in the United
States of America. In the earlier versions, Polly had in-
quired, "Can it be a Crime (in the Nature of Things I
mean) to add to the Number of the King's Subjects, in a
new Country that really wants People?" The *Journal*
changes "the King's Subjects" to "useful citizens."[17]

16. *American Law Journal*, 4 (1813), 458-60. The speech is in No. III in
Vol. IV, and the table of contents referred to here is at the beginning of No. III.
Pages 459 and 460 are erroneously numbered 359 and 360 in the copy in the
New York Public Library.

17. The text in the *American Law Journal* differs in certain other particulars
from that of the early British periodicals, but in the main it follows them
closely, even including Polly's request for a statue to her memory. Actually
it is even closer to the version of Peter Annet in his *Social Bliss Considered*
(1749). It obviously did not come from the more recent *Eccentric Biography,*
and could hardly have been copied from Carey's *American Museum* because it
followed the earlier versions in several places where Carey had not.

The impressiveness of Polly's appearance in a legal periodical is illustrated by the extraordinary effect which it had, sixty-five years later, upon the distinguished biographer, John Morley. When Morley first published his *Diderot and the Encyclopaedists* at London in 1878, he did not know that Polly's oration had been printed in the *American Law Journal*. In a chapter on Raynal's *Histoire,* he described at some length how the speech had been treated by Raynal in that work. As evidence of Raynal's "curious lightheartedness as to historic veracity," he cited Jefferson's famous anecdote in which Silas Deane tells Raynal there never was a law against bastardy in Massachusetts and in which Franklin admits authorship of the speech.[18]

Later in the same year, 1878, a new edition of Lord Morley's book came out in New York. And at the end of the preface was this paragraph:

NOTE TO THE NEW EDITION

Since the following pages were printed, an American correspondent writes to me with reference to the dialogue between Franklin and Raynal, mentioned on page 382:—"I have now before me Volume IV. of the *American Law Journal,* printed at Philadelphia in the year 1813, and at page 458 find in full, 'The Speech of Miss Polly Baker, delivered before a court of judicature in *Connecticut,* where she was prosecuted.'" Raynal, therefore, would have been right if instead of Massachusetts he had said Connecticut, and either Franklin told an untruth, or else Silas Deane.[19]

18. Morley, *Diderot,* II, 234-36.
19. This note was dated September 1878.

This remarkable note was repeated in Morley's London edition of 1886, and yet again in his London edition of 1905. Raynal had not said Massachusetts—he had said New England—but even if he had said Connecticut he still would have been wrong in representing the speech as authentic. Apparently it never occurred to Morley to doubt the authority of a publication with such a name as the *American Law Journal*.

Since Polly Baker, despite debunkers, now had managed to have her biography published on both sides of the Atlantic and had squeezed through the grim portals of a legal journal, it is not surprising to find an American historian who embraced her and welcomed her into his pages.

The historian was Charles W. Elliott. His book *The New England History* was published in two volumes in 1857. After citing the instance of one Rebecca Rawson as an example of how the course of true love did not run smooth even in New England, he wrote: "The case of Polly Baker, of Connecticut, was more curious. She was handsome, and pleasing, and was wooed and won by the son of a Magistrate. She was seduced and deserted; and when her child was born, was punished; at various times she was whipped, fined, and imprisoned. Once she spoke to the Court, in a very clear and remarkable manner." Then Elliott quoted about fourteen sentences from Polly, after which he added: "The Court discharged her without punishment for that time, the lawyers made her presents, and her seducer afterward married her."[20]

20. Elliott, *The New England History* (New York, 1857), II, 21-22.

Elliott was most unusual in one way: he cited his source. It was the 1804 Worcester edition of *Eccentric Biography*. By coincidence his very next paragraph was about Benjamin Franklin and the newspaper which he helped his brother publish in Boston. But Elliott obviously had no idea that there was any connection between Benjamin and Polly.

It is an easy jump from Charles W. Elliott into the twentieth century. In 1917 Arthur W. Calhoun published his imposing work *A Social History of the American Family*. For more than a generation this book has continued to be a standard work, used in colleges and read by people interested in sociology. In Volume I is a description of how domestic troubles were handled by the courts in colonial New England. The following quotation is from the 1945 edition: "Discretion was not always mixed with the sentences. Witness the case of Polly Baker of Connecticut who was seduced and deserted and when her child was born was punished, various times whipped, fined, and imprisoned." Then Calhoun quotes about nine sentences from Polly's speech and concludes: "The court discharged her without punishment for that time, the lawyers made her presents, and her seducer afterwards married her."[21]

Calhoun does not say where he got this information, but there can be little doubt that his source was Elliott's *The New England History*. In fact, the only change Calhoun made in the concluding sentence was to add an "s" to "afterward." At the time Calhoun wrote, the speech had been published in collections of Franklin's writings and had

21. Calhoun, *A Social History of the American Family*, rev. edn. (New York, 1945), I, 138.

been ascribed to him in numerous biographies. But all had escaped Calhoun's attention.

Nor is it likely that the end has been reached. Even in the twenty-first century, someone will surely reincarnate Polly Baker.

APPENDIX
BIBLIOGRAPHY
INDEX

APPENDIX *Comparison of Texts*

GENERAL ADVERTISER

In this column, line for line, is "The Speech of Miss Polly Baker," as printed in the *General Advertiser* in London on April 15, 1747. This is the earliest known printing.

VARIATIONS

In this column are the verbal variations found in nine other selected texts. It is NOT the purpose of this collation to show differences of punctuation, spelling, capital letters, and italics. The texts are identified thus:

GM—*Gentleman's Magazine*, April 1747.

LM—*London Magazine*, April 1747.

BPB—*Boston Weekly Post-Boy*, July 20, 1747.

MG—*Maryland Gazette*, August 11, 1747.

PA—[Peter Annet] *Social Bliss Considered* (London, 1749), pp. 99-105.

NH—*New-Haven Gazette*, April 27, 1786.

AM—*American Museum*, March 1787, 1st edition.

JP—James Parton, *Life and Times of Benjamin Franklin* (Boston, 1864), I, 219-21.

AHS—A. H. Smyth, ed., *The Writings of Benjamin Franklin* (New York, 1905-1907), II, 463-67.

The SPEECH of Miss POLLY BAKER,

before a Court of Judicature, at *Connecticut* near

Boston in *New-England*; where she was prosecuted

VARIATIONS

IN *BPB* AND *MG*, THE USUAL INTRODUCTORY PARAGRAPH IS PRECEDED BY EXPLANATIONS, THUS:

BPB *The following remarkable Speech is printed both in the* London *and* Gentleman's Magazines *for the Month of* April *last; as also in several of the* London & *other* British *late News Papers.*

MG The following very famous SPEECH has been published in the *London* and *Gentleman's Magazines* for *April* past, as well as in some other *British* Papers; but was there printed incorrectly, which I suppose was occasioned by the Mutilation it suffer'd, in passing through the Hands of Transcribers before it reach'd the Press in *London:* And happening to have a correct Copy of it by me, I cannot think it amiss to give it my Readers, not doubting it's favourable Reception.

PA BAKER, said to be delivered by her   *AM* OMIT The

BPB Con–ct-cut, N.E (OMIT near Boston in New-England)

AM in Connecticut (OMIT near Boston in New-England)

MG OMIT near Boston

PA in the Colony of Connecticut (OMIT near Boston)

NH JP Judicatory (OMIT at Connecticut near Boston)

the Fifth Time, for having a Bastard Child: Which influenced the Court to dispense with her Punishment, and induced one of her Judges to marry her the next Day.

[159]

MAY it please the Honourable Bench to indulge me in a few Words: I am a poor unhappy Woman, who have no Money to fee Lawyers to plead for me, being hard put to it to get a tolerable Living. I shall not trouble your Honours with long Speeches; for I have not the Presumption to expect, that you may, by any Means, be prevailed on to deviate in your Sentence from the Law, in my Favour. All I humbly hope is, That your Honours

NH a fifth   *IP* for a fifth   *AM* PARAGRAPH ENDS WITH Child. OUTCOME OF TRIAL MOVED TO END OF SPEECH.

NH IP AHS and which induced

GM Day, by whom she has had fifteen Children. (BUT NOT IN ALL COPIES; SEE PAGES 27-29.)

NH Day,— —by whom she had fifteen Children.

IP AHS Day—by whom she had fifteen Children.   PA FIRST OF 25 FOOTNOTES AFTER DAY.   SEE PAGES 52-56.

MG OMIT in

PA NEW PARAGRAPH   *NH IP AHS* OMIT tolerable

BPB OMIT I   *AM* nor have I the

VARIATIONS

GENERAL ADVERTISER

would charitably move the Governor's Goodness on my
AM in my

Behalf, that my Fine may be remitted. This is the Fifth
PA NEW PARAGRAPH

Time, Gentlemen, that I have been dragg'd before your

Court on the same Account; twice I have paid heavy
MG Courts   *NH JP* OMIT I

Fines, and twice have been brought to Publick Punish-

ment, for want of Money to pay those Fines. This may
AM these fines

have been agreeable to the Laws, and I don't dispute it;
BPB be agreeable   *MG* Laws; I do not

but since Laws are sometimes unreasonable in themselves,
NH JP since the laws

and therefore repealed, and others bear too hard on the

Subject in particular Circumstances; and therefore there is
NH AM JP particular instances

left a Power somewhat to dispense with the Execution of
MG NH JP AHS somewhere to dispense

them; I take the Liberty to say, That I think this Law,

by which I am punished, is both unreasonable in itself,
NH JP AHS OMIT is

[160]

and particularly severe with regard to me, who have always lived an inoffensive Life in the Neighbourhood where I was born, and defy my Enimies (if I have any) to say I ever wrong'd Man, Woman, or Child. Abstracted from the Law, I cannot conceive (may it please your Honours) what the Nature of my Offence is. I have brought Five fine Children into the World, at the Risque of my Life; I have maintain'd them well by my own Industry, without burthening the Township, and would have done it better, if it had not been for the heavy Charges and Fines I have paid. Can it be a Crime (in the Nature of Things I mean) to add to the Number of the King's Subjects, in a new Country that really wants People? I own it, I should think it a Praise-worthy, rather then a punishable Action.

[161]

AM NEW PARAGRAPH   *NH JP* have ever wronged

NH JP AHS INSERT any BEFORE Man

NH JP OMIT fine

PA and INSTEAD OF I

MG could have

PA NEW PARAGRAPH

NH JP AHS OMIT the Number of

MG OMIT it

PA OMIT FIRST a
     a Praise-worthy

MG NH JP AHS MOVE rather IN FRONT OF

GENERAL ADVERTISER

I have debauched no other Woman's Husband, nor enticed
any Youth; these Things I never was charg'd with, nor
has any one the least Cause of Complaint against me, unless, perhaps, the Minister, or Justice, because I have had
Children without being married, by which they have
missed a Wedding Fee. But, can ever this be a Fault of
mine? I appeal to your Honours. You are pleased to allow I don't want Sense; but I must be stupified to the last
Degree, not to prefer the Honourable State of Wedlock,
to the Condition I have lived in. I always was, and still
am willing to enter into it; and doubt not my behaving
well in it, having all the Industry, Frugality, Fertility,
and Skill in Oeconomy, appertaining to a good Wife's

[162]

Variations:

MG any innocent Youth   *AHS* any other youth

MG or the Justice   *NH JP AHS* ministers of justice

GM NH AM JP AHS OMIT ever   *MG* can even this

MG must be stupid   *PA* should be stupified

GM ASTERISK BEFORE Wedlock, AND FOOTNOTE SAYS: *See Maid's
Soliloquy, Jan. Mag. p. 42.

PA and am still willing

BPB OMIT and doubt not my behaving well in it
MG I INSTEAD OF and

PA fertility, skill and oeconomy appertaining

Character. I defy any Person to say, I ever refused an *NH JP AHS* any one to say
Offer of that Sort: On the contrary, I readily consented to
the only Proposal of Marriage that ever was made me,
which was when I was a Virgin; but too easily confiding
in the Person's Sincerity that made it, I unhappily lost my
own Honour, by trusting to his; for he got me with Child, *AHS* OMIT own
and then forsook me: That very Person you all know; *NH JP AHS* NEW PARAGRAPH
he is now become a Magistrate of this Country; and I *GM MG AM* this county
had Hopes he would have appeared this Day on the
Bench, and have endeavoured to moderate the Court in
my Favour; then I should have scorn'd to have mention'd
it; but I must now complain of it, as unjust and unequal,
That my Betrayer and Undoer, the first Cause of all my *BPB MG* OMIT now
Faults and Miscarriages (if they must be deemed such)

[163]

VARIATIONS

GENERAL ADVERTISER	VARIATIONS
should be advanc'd to Honour and Power in the Government, that punishes my Misfortunes with Stripes and Infamy.	MG the same Government AM that government AHS this government
I should be told, 'tis like, That were there no	MG PA AM I shall be PA NEW PARAGRAPH
Act of Assembly in the Case, the Precepts of Religion are	AM this case
violated by my Transgressions. If mine, then, is a religious Offence, leave it to religious Punishments. You	GM NH AM IP AHS OMIT then NH IP religious transgression, leave MG leave it, Gentlemen, to
have already excluded me from the Comforts of your	MG from all the
Church-Communion. Is not that sufficient? You believe	
I have offended Heaven, and must suffer eternal Fire:	
Will not that be sufficient? What Need is there, then, of	NH IP SENTENCE BEGINNING What need MOVES UP TWO LINES TO FOLLOW Is not that sufficient?
your additional Fines and Whipping? I own, I do not	MG Whippings
think as you do; for, if I thought what you call a Sin,	
was really such, I could not presumptuously commit it.	MG AM I would not

[164]

NH]P AHS crowned the whole

PA AHS NEW PARAGRAPH

MG if you, great Men,* must be (INSET NOTE SAYS: *Turning to some Gentlemen of the Assembly, then in Court.)

MG Prohibitions. Reflect a little on the horrid Consequences of this Law in particular: What Numbers of procur'd Abortions! and how many distress'd Mothers have been driven, by the Terror of Punishment and public Shame, to imbrue, contrary to Nature, their own trembling Hands in the Blood of their helpless Offspring! Nature would have induc'd them to nurse it up with a Parent's Fondness. 'Tis the Law therefore, 'tis the Law itself that is guilty of all these Barbarities and Murders. Repeal it then, Gentlemen; let it be expung'd for ever from your Books: And on the other hand, take into your (OMITTING But)

But, how can it be believed, that Heaven is angry at my having Children, when to the little done by me towards it, God has been pleased to add his Divine Skill and admirable Workmanship in the Formation of their Bodies, and crown'd it, by furnishing them with rational and immortal Souls. Forgive me, Gentlemen, if I talk a little extravagantly on these Matters; I am no Divine, but if you, Gentlemen, must be making Laws, do not turn natural and useful Actions into Crimes, by your Prohibitions.

[165]

But take into your wise Consideration, the great and

GENERAL ADVERTISER

VARIATIONS

GENERAL ADVERTISER	VARIATIONS
growing Number of Batchelors in the Country, many of	*PA* in this country
whom from the mean Fear of the Expences of a Family,	*MG* Expence
have never sincerely and honourably courted a Woman in	
their Lives; and by their Manner of Living, leave unpro-	
duced (which is little better than Murder) Hundreds of	*MG* which I think is
their Posterity to the Thousandth Generation. Is not this a	*MG* Is not theirs a
greater Offence against the Publick Good, than mine?	
Compel them, then, by Law, either to Marriage, or to pay	*MG* by a Law, either to Marry, or pay
	AM either to marry
double the Fine of Fornication every Year. What must	*AM* What shall
poor young Women do, whom Custom have forbid to solicit	*BPB* omit young
	GM AM custom hath forbid *LM MG PA* has forbid
	NH custom and nature forbid
	JP AHS customs and nature forbid
the Men, and who cannot force themselves upon Husbands,	
when the Laws take no Care to provide them any; and yet	*BPB* omit them

[166]

severely punish them if they do their Duty without them; the Duty of the first and great Command of Nature, and of Nature's God, *Encrease and Multiply.* A Duty, from the steady Performance of which, nothing has been able to deter me; but for its Sake, I have hazarded the Loss of the Publick Esteem, and have frequently endured Publick Disgrace and Punishment; and therefore ought, in my humble Opinion, instead of a Whipping, to have a Statue erected to my Memory.

[167]

MG punish if they do their Duty without them? Yes, Gentlemen, I venture to call it a Duty; 'tis the Duty of the first

AM the first great   *AHS* OMIT FINAL of

MG has ever been

MG and frequently incurr'd

AM OMIT and Punishment

PA OMIT to

AM This judicious address influenced the court to dispense with her punishment, and induced one of her judges to marry her next day. She supported an irreproachable character, and had fifteen children by her husband.
  N. B. Another account says her name was Sarah Olitor.

I. Chronological List of Printed Texts
of Polly Baker's Speech

British Periodicals in 1747

1. *The General Advertiser* (London), No. 3889, April 15, 1747. Earliest known printing. British Museum.

2. *The St. James's Evening Post* (London), No. 5810, April 16, 1747. Very nearly identical with No. 1. Yale University Library.

3. *The London Evening-Post* (London), No. 3034, April 16, 1747. Presumably taken from No. 1, though there are minor changes. New-York Historical Society.

4. *Old England: or, The Broadbottom Journal* (London), No. 153, April 18, 1747. Source probably No. 1. New-York Historical Society.

5. *The Westminster Journal. Or, New Weekly Miscellany* (London), No. 281, April 18, 1747. Identical in language with No. 1. British Museum.

6. *The Kentish Post; or, The Canterbury News Letter*

(Canterbury), No. 3072, April 18, 1747. Practically identical with No. 1. British Museum.

7. *The Penny London Post, or, the Morning Advertiser* (London), No. 620, April 20, 1747. Only a few trivial changes from earlier texts. Some kinship with No. 4. Library of Congress.

8. *The Bath Journal* (Bath), No. 165 (Vol. IV, No. 4), April 20, 1747. Almost certainly copied from No. 3. Library of Congress.

9. *The Northampton Mercury* (Northampton). Text, Vol. XXVIII, No. III, April 20, 1747. Almost certainly copied from No. 3. "An Answer to Polly Baker's Speech," May 11, 1747. Both numbers in British Museum.

10. *Pue's Occurrences* (Dublin), Vol. XLVI, No. 30, April 25, 1747. Very close kinship with No. 3. British Museum.

11. *The Chester Courant* (Chester), apparently April 27, 1747. Unavailable, but see No. 22, below. Text almost identical with No. 3.

12. *The Gentleman's Magazine* (London). Text, 17 (April 1747), 175-76 (issued about May 1). Source could be No. 1, but there are a few changes. Examined in many libraries. "Myra" epigram, *ibid.,* 194. "William Smith" letter, 17 (May 1747), 211. "L. Americanus" letter, 17 (June 1747), 295. Apology to Paul Dudley, 18 (July 1748), 332. Query from reader, 51 (1781), 367.

13. *The London Magazine* (London), 16 (April 1747), 178-79. Almost identical with No. 1. Examined in several libraries.

14. *The British Magazine* (London), 2 (April 1747), 154-56. Identical in language with No. 1. University of Chicago Library. Should not be confused with *British Magazine,* Edinburgh.

15. *The Scots Magazine* (Edinburgh). Text, 9 (April 1747), 177-78. Apparently taken from No. 12. "Myra" epigram, 168. Harvard College Library and New York Public Library.

16. *The London Magazine: and Monthly Chronologer* (Dublin). Text, April 1747, 172-73. Apparently taken from No. 13. New York Public Library. "Myra" epigram, 182. Binder's title: "Exshaw's Magazine."

American Periodicals in 1747

17. *The Boston Weekly Post-Boy* (Boston), No. 661, July 20, 1747. Only trivial changes from British periodicals. Perhaps a little closer to No. 1 than to other British sources listed. Massachusetts Historical Society.

18. *The New-York Gazette, Revived in the Weekly Post-Boy* (New York), No. 237, Aug. 3, 1747. Unquestionably from No. 17. New-York Historical Society.

19. *The New-York Weekly Journal* (New York), No. 711, Aug. 3, 1747. Unquestionably from No. 17. New-York Historical Society.

20. *The Maryland Gazette* (Annapolis), No. 120, Aug. 11, 1747. Source mysterious. Some kinship with Nos. 4 and 7, but contains passages appearing nowhere else. Hall of Records, Annapolis.

Bibliography

Other Eighteenth-Century Printings

21. [Peter Annet], *Social Bliss Considered: In Marriage and Divorce; Cohabiting unmarried, and Public Whoring* (London, 1749), 99-105. "By Gideon Archer" appears on title page of book. Text of speech perhaps from No. 13, conceivably from Nos. 1 or 14. Annet annotates text with 25 footnotes. Vassar College Library.

22. *The Chester Miscellany, Being a Collection of Several Pieces Both in Prose and Verse Which Were in the Chester Courant from January 1745-May 1750* (Chester, Eng., 1750), 223-26. Text reprinted from No. 11. British Museum.

23. [Peter Annet], *A Collection of the Tracts of a Certain Free Enquirer, Noted by His Sufferings for His Opinions* (London? 1766?), 255-59. Harvard College Library. *Social Bliss Considered* (No. 21) is one of the tracts in this book.

24. *Posten* (Stockholm), 1768, No. 46. Swedish translation. Source given as *London Magazine* (No. 13). I have not seen *Posten,* but it is mentioned by J. V. Johansson (No. 48, below), 178n and 203.

25. [Guillaume-Thomas Raynal], *Histoire Philosophique et Politique, Des Établissements & du Commerce des Européens dans les Deux Indes* (Amsterdam, 1770), VI, 257-62. Harvard College Library. The speech, in French translation, is perhaps derived from one of the English magazines or from Annet (Nos. 21 or 23). Raynal's work had major revisions in 1774 and 1780 and was issued in a great many editions (some translated into other languages), which I cannot at-

tempt to cite separately in this list. Raynal's by-line was not in the first edition but appeared in many later ones. The speech, with comments on it, is in the section on New England in Book 17.

26. *The Essex Gazette* (Salem, Mass.), No. 238, Feb. 16, 1773. Source uncertain. New York Public Library.

27. *The Virginia Gazette* (Williamsburg), No. 1131, April 1, 1773. Reprinted from No. 26 with acknowledgment. Boston Public Library.

28. *The History of North America* (London, 1776), 82-87. The speech is an English translation of Raynal's French translation (No. 25), though the book does not say so. Library of Congress.

29. *Courier Politique et Littéraire, Annonces et Avis Divers: Or, French Evening Post* (London), Vol. I, No. 8 (June 17, 1777), 60-61. French translation. Source uncertain. Harvard College Library.

30. *Courier de l'Europe* (London), Vol. II, No. V (June 17, 1777), 40. Same French translation as in No. 29. Yale University Library.

31. [J. P. Brissot de Warville], *Bibliothèque Philosophique du Législateur, du Politique, du Jurisconsulte* (Berlin, 1782), VIII, 363-68. French translation. Source uncertain. Text and comments. Library of Congress.

32. *The Hampshire Herald: or, the Weekly Advertiser* (Springfield, Mass.), No. 170, Aug. 9, 1785. Numerous unimportant differences between this and early English texts. Source uncertain. Library of Congress.

33. *The New-Haven Gazette, and the Connecticut Magazine* (New Haven), 1 (April 27, 1786), 86-87. Many differences between this and early English texts. Source uncertain. Yale University Library.

34. *The American Museum* (Philadelphia), 1 (March 1787), 243-45, first edition. Fairly close to *Gentleman's Magazine* (No. 12), but source uncertain. Massachusetts Historical Society. Later editions of the March number will not be listed separately.

35. *Patrioten* (Stockholm), 1793 volume, 302-6. Swedish translation from Raynal's French translation. I have not seen this newspaper, but it is mentioned by J. V. Johansson (No. 48, below), 178n.

36. *The Edinburgh Magazine, or Literary Miscellany* (Edinburgh), New Ser., 3 (April 1794), 288-94. The speech is given as part of an essay entitled "Interesting Reflections on the Life of Miss Polly Baker." Source of text unknown. The whole essay shows signs of being from some undiscovered London periodical. Hamilton College Library, Clinton, N.Y. This magazine should not be confused with *The Edinburgh Magazine, and Literary Miscellany*.

37. *The New-York Magazine; or, Literary Repository* (New York), 6 (January 1795), 39-46. This magazine merely reprinted the "Interesting Reflections" just mentioned. Yale University Library.

38. *The Philadelphia Monthly Magazine* (Philadelphia), 1 (June 1798), 325-27. Apparently taken from No. 34. Library of Congress.

Nineteenth Century

39. *Eccentric Biography; or, Memoirs of Remarkable Female Characters, Ancient and Modern* [London, 1803], 11-16. This book reprinted part of the "Interesting Reflections" (see Nos. 36 and 37). Harvard College Library.

40. *Eccentric Biography,* etc. (Worcester, Mass., April 1804), 18-23. This is an American edition of No. 39. A second American edition came out at Worcester in 1805. Copies of both American editions are in Houghton Library, Harvard.

41. *The American Law Journal* (Baltimore), 4 (1813), 458-60. Text has considerable kinship with Annet's (Nos. 21 and 23) and may have come from there directly or indirectly. New York Public Library.

42. [M. de l'Espinasse, Chevalier de Langeac], *Anecdotes Anglaises et Américaines* (Paris, 1813), II, 130-39. Text is in same French translation found in Nos. 29 and 30, though with certain changes near the end. Speech is followed by anecdote revealing authorship. Library of Congress.

43. James Parton, *Life and Times of Benjamin Franklin* (Boston, 1864). Text and comments, I, 219-21. Other references, II, 400, 417-18, 646. Parton said the speech was in the *Pennsylvania Gazette,* and cited no other source for his text. Actually the speech was not in that paper, and Parton's version is practically identical with that of the *New-Haven Gazette* (No. 33).

44. *The Complete Works of Benjamin Franklin,* ed. John Bigelow (New York, 1887), II, 18-22. Text is from No. 43.

Bibliography

Twentieth Century

45. *The Writings of Benjamin Franklin,* ed. Albert Henry Smyth (New York, 1905-1907). Text and comments, II, 463-67. Other references, I, 172-73. Smyth said he was reprinting the speech from the *Gentleman's Magazine* (No. 12), but he obviously did not. His text is very like Parton's (No. 43), but is not from that source exclusively.

46. *Frankfurter Zeitung* (Frankfurt, Germany), Sept. 15, 1912. German translation by Pierre de la Juillière, from the French translation used by Denis Diderot. I have not seen the German newspaper but it is cited by J. V. Johansson (No. 48, below), 60, and by Herbert Dieckmann (No. 58, below), xxv.

47. Johan Viktor Johansson, "Raynal, Diderot och Polly Baker," *Göteborgs Högskolas årsskrift,* 26 (1920), 2. Apparently this article contains Polly's speech in an early English version and also as G. T. Raynal and Denis Diderot used it. I have not seen the article, but Johansson mentions it in the book described below (No. 48), 187n, 202.

48. Johan Viktor Johansson, *Études sur Denis Diderot* (Göteborg et Paris, 1927). At pp. 87-92 Johansson gives Diderot's French version of the speech, and at pp. 167-73 he gives the *London Magazine* text (No. 13) with the variations of the *Gentleman's Magazine* (No. 12), *American Museum* (No. 34), Parton (No. 43), and Bigelow (No. 44).

49. *Benjamin Franklin on Marriage* (Larchmont, N.Y.: Peter Pauper Press, 1929), 35-43. Source perhaps Smyth (No. 45).

[175]

50. Denis Diderot, *Supplément au Voyage de Bougain-ville,* ed. Gilbert Chinard (Paris et Baltimore, 1935). Diderot's French text of the speech, 155-59. Other references, 7, 154-60.

51. *Satires and Hoaxes of Benjamin Franklin* (Mount Vernon, N.Y.: Peter Pauper Press, 1935), 14-19. Text very like Smyth (No. 45).

52. Frank Luther Mott and Chester E. Jorgenson, *Benjamin Franklin* (New York, 1936), 190-93 with brief note. Credited to *Gentleman's Magazine* (No. 12) but evidently taken from Smyth (No. 45), who said he copied it from *Gentleman's Magazine* but did not.

53. *Dr. Benjamin Franklin and the Ladies* (Mount Vernon, N.Y.: Peter Pauper Press, 1939), 62-65. Text very like Smyth (No. 45).

54. *The Autobiography of Benjamin Franklin,* "with Sayings of Poor Richard, Hoaxes, Bagatelles, Essays and Letters," selected by Carl Van Doren (Pocket Books, Inc., New York, 1940), 229-32. Credited to *Gentleman's Magazine* (No. 12) but evidently taken from Smyth (No. 45), who said he copied it from *Gentleman's Magazine* but did not.

55. *American Issues,* ed. Willard Thorp, Merle Curti, and Carlos Baker (Chicago, 1941), I, 44-45. Apparently taken from Smyth (No. 45).

56. *A Benjamin Franklin Reader,* ed. Nathan G. Goodman (New York, 1945), 723-25. Apparently taken from Smyth (No. 45).

57. *Diderot: Selected Philosophical Writings,* ed. J. Lough (Cambridge, Eng., 1953), 185-87. Lough reprinted

the French text of Diderot's *Supplément,* including
Polly's speech, from Chinard (No. 50).

58. Denis Diderot, *Supplément au Voyage de Bougain-
ville,* ed. Herbert Dieckmann (Genève, Librairie
Droz; Lille, Librairie Giard, 1955), 36-38. Diderot's
French version of the speech, with notes.

59. *The Benjamin Franklin Sampler,* copyright by Nathan
G. Goodman (New York: Fawcett Publications,
1956), 231-34. Apparently taken from Smyth (No.
45).

II. Alphabetical List of Works Containing
Speech or Mentioning Polly

NOTE: Very few writers have dealt at any considerable
length with the affair of Polly Baker. By far the most
thorough and informative was the Swede, Johan Viktor
Johansson, who published his findings in Swedish and
French in the 1920's. In 1899, Howard Payson Arnold
produced a free-wheeling chapter of about ten pages. In
1957, Alfred Owen Aldridge gave us a helpful chapter on
Polly's career in France. There are brief comments in
many other works, perhaps the most interesting being those
of Parton, Smyth, and Van Doren. Some of the works
cited below contain only passing references, and some are
sadly inaccurate. Works containing the text of the speech
have already been listed chronologically but will also be
found in abbreviated form in the alphabetical list below,
along with the key numbers which they bear in the chronological list.

Adams, Charles Francis, ed., *The Works of John Adams* (Boston, 1856), I, 319.

Adams, John, letter to James Warren from Paris, April 13, 1783, *Warren-Adams Letters,* II (Massachusetts Historical Society, *Collections,* 73 [1925]), 209.

Adams, John, Autobiography (unpublished), Adams Microfilm Reel 180. The reference is under date of May 27, 1778, but likely was inserted later.

Aldridge, Alfred Owen, *Franklin and His French Contemporaries* (New York, 1957), Chap. 6, "Polly Baker," 95-104.

Aldridge, Alfred Owen, "Franklin's Deistical Indians," American Philosophical Society, *Proceedings,* 94 (1950), 403.

American Issues. See No. 55 in chronological list.

American Law Journal. See No. 41.

American Museum. See No. 34.

Annet, Peter. See Nos. 21 and 23.

Arnold, Howard Payson, *Historic Side-lights* (New York, 1899), 141-51.

Balzac, Honoré de, *A Distinguished Provincial in Paris,* trans. Ellen Marriage (Vol. VIII of Illustrated Library Edition of Balzac's works, Boston and New York, no date), 209-10. This novel was first published in 1839.

[Barlow, Joel], translator's note in J. P. Brissot de Warville, *New Travels in the United States of America* (London and Dublin edns., 1792), 330-31; (New York edn., 1792), 182.

Bath Journal. See No. 8.

Bell, Whitfield J., Jr., editorial note in Benjamin Franklin,

The Old Mistresses' Apologue (Philadelphia, 1956), next to last page.

Benjamin Franklin on Marriage. See No. 49.

Benjamin Franklin Reader. See No. 56.

Benjamin Franklin Sampler. See No. 59.

Bigelow, John, ed. *Complete Works of Benjamin Franklin.* See No. 44.

Bigelow, John, *The Life of Benjamin Franklin, Written by Himself,* 4th edn., revised and corrected (Philadelphia, 1900), III, 300.

Boston Weekly Post-Boy. See No. 17.

Brissot de Warville, J. P., *Bibliothèque Philosophique.* See No. 31.

Brissot de Warville, J. P., *New Travels.* See Barlow, Joel.

British Magazine. See No. 14.

Broadbottom Journal. See No. 4.

Bruce, William Cabell, *Benjamin Franklin Self-Revealed,* 2nd edn. (New York, 1923), II, 467-68.

Calhoun, Arthur W., *A Social History of the American Family* (New York edn., 1945), I, 138. First issued 1917.

Canterbury News Letter. See No. 6.

Chester Courant. See No. 11.

Chester Miscellany. See No. 22.

Chinard, Gilbert. See No. 50.

Commager, Henry Steele, "Franklin Still Speaks to Us," *New York Times Magazine,* Jan. 15, 1956, 74.

Courier de l'Europe. See No. 30.

Courier Politique et Littéraire. See No. 29.

Crane, Verner W., *Benjamin Franklin's Letters to the Press, 1758-1775* (Chapel Hill, 1950), xviii, xxv.

Diderot, Denis, his version of Polly Baker's speech, written about 1780 but not published until the twentieth century. Especially see Nos. 48, 50, and 58. Also see Nos. 46, 47, and 57.

Dieckmann, Herbert, *Inventaire du Fonds Vandeul et Inédits de Diderot* (Genève, 1951), 26-27, 144-45.

Dieckmann, Herbert, ed. Diderot's *Supplément*. See No. 58.

Dr. Benjamin Franklin and the Ladies. See No. 53.

Eccentric Biography. See Nos. 39 and 40.

Edinburgh Magazine. See No. 36.

Elie, Rudolph, "The Roving Eye," *Boston Herald,* Dec. 4, 1951.

Elliott, Charles W., *The New England History* (New York, 1857), II, 21-22.

Essex Gazette. See No. 26.

"Exshaw's Magazine." See No. 16.

Faÿ, Bernard, *Bibliographie Critique des Ouvrages Français Relatifs aux États-Unis, 1770-1800* (Paris, 1925), 45-46.

Faÿ, Bernard, *Franklin, the Apostle of Modern Times* (Boston, 1929), 205, 206.

Feugère, Anatole, *Un Précurseur de la Révolution: L'Abbé Raynal* (Angoulême, 1922), 4-5, 217-19.

Fisher, Sydney George, *The True Benjamin Franklin* (Philadelphia, 1898), 139-41. Fisher quotes most of the speech, perhaps from Parton (No. 43) or Bigelow (No. 44). In the third edition, published in 1926, Polly is mentioned at pp. 3-4, 139-41.

Ford, Paul Leicester, *Franklin Bibliography* (Brooklyn, 1889), 289.

Frankfurter Zeitung. See No. 46.

Franklin, William, manuscript letter to Jonathan Williams, dated London, July 30, 1807. Indiana University Library.

General Advertiser. See No. 1.

Gentleman's Magazine. See No. 12.

Goodman, Nathan G. See Nos. 56 and 59.

Hall, Lieut. Francis, *Travels in Canada, and the United States, in 1816 and 1817,* 2nd edn. (London, 1819), 296-97; (Boston, 1818), 229-30. Also see Nevins, Allan.

Hampshire Herald. See No. 32.

Hirn, Yrjö, "Polly Baker," *Nya Argus,* 1913, 19. Reprinted in *Episoder* (Stockholm), 1918, 214 ff. I have not seen either periodical; they are cited by Johansson (No. 48), 184, 201.

History of North America. See No. 28.

Hone, William. See *Table Book.*

Hughes, Rupert, "Washington, Franklin, Adams, Hamilton, Jefferson," in *American Writers on American Literature,* ed. John Macy (New York, 1931), 45.

Jefferson, Thomas, anecdote on Franklin's revealing authorship of the speech. Jefferson enclosed the anecdote with a letter to Robert Walsh, Dec. 4, 1818. The manuscript is in the Library of Congress. Printed, among other places, in *The Writings of Thomas Jefferson,* ed. H. A. Washington (Washington, D.C., 1854), VIII, 501-2; and *The Writings of Thomas Jefferson,* ed. Paul Leicester Ford (New York, 1899), X, 120-21.

Johansson, Johan Viktor, *Études sur Denis Diderot.* See No. 48.

Johansson, Johan Viktor, "Raynal, Diderot och Polly Baker." See No. 47.

Jorgenson, Chester E. See No. 52.

Juillière, Pierre de la. See No. 46.

Justamond, J. O., translator's note in a number of English editions of Raynal's *Histoire,* published in London under the title *A Political and Philosophical History of the Settlements and Trade of the Europeans in the East and West Indies.* For example, 1777 edn., V, 188; and 1788 edn., VII, 244-45. Justamond explains why he omitted Polly's speech.

Kentish Post. See No. 6.

Langeac, Chevalier de. See No. 42.

Life, October 5, 1959, 119-20.

London Evening-Post. See No. 3.

London Magazine (Dublin). See No. 16.

London Magazine (London). See No. 13.

Lough, J. See No. 57.

Maryland Gazette. See No. 20.

[Mazzei, Philip], *Recherches Historiques et Politiques sur les États-Unis de l'Amérique Septentrionale* (Paris, 1788), III, 23-25.

McMaster, John Bach, *Benjamin Franklin As a Man of Letters* (Boston, 1887), 70-71, 271-72.

[Morellet, Abbé André], unpublished commonplace book, British Museum, Additional Manuscripts 6134, folio 57b.

Morley, John, *Diderot and the Encyclopaedists* (London, 1878), II, 234-36. This passage on Polly Baker in Morley's chapter on Raynal remained in later editions. Besides, Polly was the subject of a "Note to the New Edition," inserted in the New York edition of 1878, p. vi, and repeated in the London editions of 1886 and 1905.

Mott, Frank Luther. See No. 52.

Nevins, Allan, ed., *America through British Eyes* (New York, 1948), 72. Excerpt reprinted from Hall, Francis.

New-Haven Gazette. See No. 33.

New-York Gazette, Revived in the Weekly Post-Boy. See No. 18.

New-York Magazine. See No. 37.

New-York Weekly Journal. See No. 19.

Northampton Mercury. See No. 9.

Old England. See No. 4.

Parton, James. See No. 43.

Patrioten. See No. 35.

Penny London Post. See No. 7.

Perrine, William, *Philadelphia Evening Bulletin,* Dec. 19, 1899.

Philadelphia Evening Bulletin. See Perrine.

Philadelphia Monthly Magazine. See No. 38.

Philobiblion, The, a Monthly Bibliographical Journal (New York), Vol. I, No. 1 (December 1861), 24; and Vol. I, No. 2 (January 1862), 44-46. In response to a question, "D.W.F." Williamsburgh, N.Y., discusses the speech and quotes from Annet's text (No. 21). "D.W.F." was not sure whether Franklin was the author.

Posten. See No. 24.

Pue's Occurrences. See No. 10.

Raynal, Abbé G. T. See No. 25.

Rolfe, Christopher, "Ben Franklin's Polly Baker," the *Mentor,* 11 (June 1923), 38-39.

Russell, Phillips, *Benjamin Franklin, the First Civilized American* (New York, 1926), 111-15, 170. Russell quotes most of the speech, apparently from Smyth (No. 45).

Bibliography

Sabin, Joseph, *A Dictionary of Books Relating to America* (New York, 1868), I, 209.

St. James's Evening Post. See No. 2.

Satires and Hoaxes of Benjamin Franklin. See No. 51.

Scots Magazine. See No. 15.

Smyth, Albert Henry. See No. 45.

Table Book, The (London), 1 (1827), 89. Reprinted London, 1866, 45. The editor of this periodical was William Hone.

Torrey, Norman L., *Voltaire and the English Deists* (New Haven, 1930), 187.

Twynam, Ella, *Peter Annet—1693-1769* (London, 194-?), 5.

Van Doren, Carl, *Benjamin Franklin* (New York, 1938), 153-55, 721-22.

Van Doren, Carl, paperback containing text of speech. See No. 54.

Virginia Gazette. See No. 27.

Voltaire, *Oeuvres Complètes de Voltaire* (Kehl, 1785), XXXVII, 277. To find the passage in subsequent editions of Voltaire's works, see article on "Ana, Anecdotes," in *Philosophical Dictionary.*

Westminster Journal. See No. 5.

Writings of Benjamin Franklin. See No. 45.

INDEX

(For the definitive list of printed texts of the Polly Baker speech and the works containing mention of it, see the Bibliography, p. 168. As Polly Baker has appeared on nearly every page of the foregoing text, the name will not be found in the Index.)

Abraham, 91-92

Adam and Eve, 29

Adams, Charles Francis, 107-8

Adams, John, on Raynal, 59; praised by Washington, 77; on Franklin's fame, 79-80, 126; attacks Polly, 90, 108; grandson attacks Polly, 107-8; mentioned, 7

Addison, Joseph, on seducers, 8-9; on female orators, 9, 112; *Cato,* 29-31; influences Franklin, 99-100

"Advice to a Young Man on the Choice of a Mistress," 105-7

Aldridge, Alfred Owen, help acknowledged, vii; views on Polly, 103

American Antiquarian Society, 27

American Law Journal, 149-52

American Museum, 138-42; variations in Polly text, 157-67

American Philosophical Society, 27

American Revolution, Raynal and Paine, 78-79; Polly placed in, 134; mentioned, 109, 132

Americanus, L., 37, 44-45, 89

American Weekly Mercury, 119

Anatomist, 19*n*

Anecdotes, Raynal's, 60-61; errors in Jefferson's, 81-87; Morellet's, 87-89; Voltaire exposes, 128-29

Anecdotes Anglaises et Américaines, 134

Annapolis, Md., speech printed in, 39-41, 120-21; mentioned, 4, 38

Annet, Peter, philosophy and career,

49-50, 56, 111; *Social Bliss,* 51-52; *Collection of Tracts,* 51*n*, 57; treatment of Polly, 52-56; variations in Polly text, 157-67; mentioned, 61, 150*n*

"Answer to Polly Baker's Speech," 33-34

"Apology for Printers," 86*n*

Apology to Paul Dudley, text of, 43

Archer, Gideon, 51

Arnold, Howard Payson, 46*n*, 104-5

Azores, 137

Bachelors, attacked by Polly, 6; attacked by Henry Baker, 12; deleted from Raynal's book, 65, 72-73; Franklin and Henry Baker, 102-3

Baker, Abijah, 98

Baker, Grace, 98

Baker, Henry, 11-12, 100-3; mentioned, 13

Baker, Polly. *See note,* at beginning of Index

Baltimore, Md., 150

Balzac, Honoré de, 136

Barlow, Joel, 133, 136

Barnes, Jack C., help acknowledged, vii, 90*n*, 138*n*, 148*n*

Bath Journal, 19

Beaumarchais, Caron de, 128

Beckford, Mr., praised in essay, 147

Beggar's Opera, 10, 100

Belcher, Jonathan, 47

Bell, Whitfield J., Jr., help acknowl-

Index

Index

Index

Florence, Italy, 130

Fornication, laws, 80, 81-83, 109; Eleonor Kellog's trials, 94-98; other New England trials, 98-99, 112, 141; Franklin's knowledge of trials, 97-99; Green's attack on law, 121-23; mentioned, 36, 46*n*, 69

Foxcroft, John, 109*n*

Frankfurter Zeitung, 69-70

Franklin and French Contemporaries, 103

Franklin, Benjamin, hoaxes besides Polly, 18, 91-93, 113; suppresses Polly speech, 39, 83-87; Green, 40, 120-23; Dudley, 46-47, 88-90; role in *1777* printing of speech, 64-65; Brissot, 73; Raynal and Americans, 76-79; Paine, 78-79; his fame, 79-80; reveals authorship to Raynal, 79-81; evidence of authorship from —Jefferson, 80-81; Morellet, 87-88; Adams, 90; William Franklin, 90; by style, 91; from background and reading, 93, 94-112; New England fornication cases, 97-99; English writers, 99-104; his philoprogenitiveness, 102-3; date of Polly's composition, 103-7; his character and Polly, 107-8; his "motives" in writing speech, 108-12 (especially 111-12); his deism, 111; bitter letter to Priestley, 112-13; role in Polly's London advent, 114-16; Breintnall, 119; motives for not publicly acknowledging Polly, 123-25; authorship revealed in print, 126-36; Voltaire, 126-29; Mazzei, 130-32; revivals of Polly after *1785,* 137-54; Carey, 138-41; mentioned re *1747* or earlier, 4, 7, 17, 26, 39, 52; mentioned, 22, 117, 118, 137, 153. *See also* note, p. 185, at beginning of Index

Franklin, Deborah, 86, 109

Franklin, James, 46, 52, 90

Franklin, Sally, 122

Franklin, Temple, 127

Franklin, William, 86, 90, 109-10

Frederick the Great, 80, 93

Free Enquirer (Annet), 51*n*, 57

Freeman, Mary, 121

French Revolution, and Raynal, 60, 75; and Brissot, 73, 75

Garlick, Richard Cecil, Jr., 131, 132*n*

Gay, John, 10, 100

Gazetteer (London), 16*n*, 124-25

Gazette Nationale, ou Le Moniteur Universal, 88*n*

General Advertiser, introduces Polly, 3, 4, 16-17; reprinted in Canterbury, 19; and *Gentleman's Magazine,* 24; and Annet, 52; the earliest known printing, 85; mystery of Polly's advent, 114-16; full text of speech, 157-67

General Evening Post, 18*n*

General Magazine (Franklin's), 85

Genesis, Franklin's hoax of, 91-92

Gentleman's Magazine, early history and imitators, 20-24; reprints Polly's speech, 22, 24, 25-32; Polly's "fifteen children," 25-29, 75; William Smith letter, 34-35, 42, 88-90; L. Americanus letter, 37; apologizes to Dudley, 43-44; not Smyth's source, 84-85, 85*n*; and *American Museum,* 140-41; variations in Polly text, 157-67; mentioned, 4, 26, 38, 40, 41, 44, 52, 58, 70, 100-1

Germany, and Polly, 69-70

Gibbon, Edward, 59

Girondists, and Brissot, 73

Godiva, Lady, 149

Green, Jonas, 40-41, 120-23

Gulliver's Travels, 124

Hackabout, Mary, 13

Haiti, and Polly, 61

Hall, David, 116, 117

Hall, Francis, 134-35, 136

Hall, John E., 150

Hamilton, Alexander, 7

Hamlin, William, 98

Hampshire Herald, 137-38

Hance, John, 121

Index

Harlotry. *See* Prostitutes
"Harlot's Progress," 13, 100
Hartford County, Conn., 98, 141
Harvard University, acknowledgment, vii; library, viii, 28-29; Dudley, 36
Henry, Patrick, 130
Henry, William, 92
Histoire Philosophique et Politique, described, 59-61; treatment of Polly, 61-62, 65-66, 72-73; translated in Britain, 62-63; language similar to Diderot's, 68; on Americans, 76-78; discussed in Franklin's house, 79, 80; Franklin's views on, 125; Voltaire exposes, 128-29; Morley changes mind, 151-52. *See also* Raynal
History of North America, 62
Hoaxes by Franklin, 18, 91-93, 113
Hodges, T. M., 143*n*
Hogarth, William, 13, 100
Hone, William, 135-36
Hughes, Rupert, 104
Hurd, Hannah, 98
Huske, E., 39

"Increase and multiply," Polly's battle cry, 6-7; Henry Baker's petitioners, 12; "Maid's Soliloquy," 29-31; Franklin and Baker, 101; Franklin to Mme. Brillon, 101-2; omitted in *Eccentric Biography,* 149
Indians, American, Raynal on, 76; Franklin's deistical, 92; Franklin's scalp hoax, 93, 113; massacred by white men, 122
Industrial Revolution, 8
"Interesting Reflections on the Life of Miss Polly Baker," 143-48
Ipswich, Mass., 44
Ireland. *See* Dublin

Jefferson, Thomas, his reply to Raynal, 77-78; his Polly anecdote, 79-80, 135, 136; errors in his anecdote, 81-87; anecdote stirs up storm, 107-8; and Mazzei, 130-32; and Francis Hall, 135; mentioned, 7, 151
Jesuits, and Raynal, 59

Joan of Arc, 149
Johansson, J. V., 15*n*, 66-67, 70-72
Johnson, Samuel, and *Gentleman's Magazine,* 21; possible connection with Polly, 25, 29; and Raynal, 59
Jones, John, 98
Joseph Andrews, 14, 111-12
Journalism. *See* Magazines, Newspapers
Junto, Franklin's club, 110, 118-19
Justamond, J. O., 62-63

Kehl, Germany, 128-29
Kellog, Eleonor, her trials, 94-98; and date of Polly's composition, 97-98, 104, 105; no happy ending, 107
Kentish Post, 19
Kottemann, Jack F., 143*n*

L. Americanus, letter defending Dudley, 37, 44-45, 89
Langeac, Chevalier de, 133-34, 135-36
Leeds, Titan, 91
Leibnitz, G. W., 80
Leningrad (St. Petersburg), 66-67, 70-71
Letter to the Abbé Raynal, 78-79
Library Company of Philadelphia, 28, 118
Library of Congress, acknowledgment, viii; British papers, 20; Polly's "fifteen children," 28-29
Life and Times of Benjamin Franklin, 108
Lillo, George, writes new kind of play, 12-13; and middle class, 15*n*; and Dudley, 47; impresses Diderot, 67; and Franklin, 100
Little Britain, 17
Livingston, Robert R., 78
London, newspapers and Polly, 16-19; magazines and Polly, 20-23; Polly's revival there, 62-65; how speech originally got there, 114-20
London Chronicle, 115
London Courant, 16*n*
London Evening-Post, 18, 19
London Gazette, 16-17, 18*n*

Index

Index

Index

Index

THIS BOOK

*was composed and printed by the Seeman Printery,
Incorporated, Durham, N. C. The typeface is
Linotype Granjon. The binding was done by The
Carolina Ruling and Binding Company, Charlotte,
N. C. The designer was Richard Stinely.*